D0909424

SOCIAL SECURITY: UNIVERSAL OR SELECTIVE?

Sixth in the fifth series of Rational Debate Seminars sponsored by the American Enterprise Institute held at The Madison Hotel Washington, D.C.

PETER LISAGOR
Moderator

SOCIAL SECURITY: UNIVERSAL OR SELECTIVE?

Wilbur J. Cohen

Milton Friedman

RATIONAL DEBATE SEMINARS

American Enterprise Institute
for Public Policy Research
Washington, D.C.

© Copyright 1972 by the
American Enterprise Institute for Public Policy Research
1150 17th Street, N.W., Washington, D.C. 20036
All rights reserved under International and
Pan-American Copyright Conventions

HD
7/25
.C 56

Library of Congress Catalog Card Number 72–77460

FOREWORD

How to provide for the aged, the disabled, and the dependent is a problem in every society. Many are the proposals, but a lasting solution is elusive. The American social security system was devised during the great depression of the 1930s as one way to meet the problem. It has wide acceptance. Yet, it is being increasingly questioned—by some for inequities and insufficiencies that have resulted as its welfare features have been expanded, and by others because this expansion has not been carried far enough. Some experts doubt that the present program can be changed to meet growing social and economic complexities.

Professor Cohen finds that the social security system "is certainly not the only way . . . and certainly not the final answer. But it is a reasonably good approach for this economy, and one which is susceptible to incremental improvements over time as our productivity and gross national product increase."

Professor Friedman may capsulize the divergence of solutions, when he says, "The fundamental issue is: as we look toward the future, do we want our society to develop in such a way that individuals separately will have greater responsibility or do we want it to develop

ALMA COLLEGE
MONTEITH LIBRARY
ALMA, MICHIGAN

in such a way that the collective entity is more dominant and more omnipresent?"

This Rational Debate between Wilbur Cohen, former Secretary of Health, Education, and Welfare, and Dr. Milton Friedman, a leader of the "Chicago School" of economics, pits one of the principal architects of social security against one of its most articulate critics.

March 1972

William J. Baroody
President
American Enterprise Institute
for Public Policy Research

CONTENTS

FIRST LECTURE

WILBUR J. COHEN

I

There are social security systems today in some 100 countries of the world. They come in all sizes, shapes, and dimensions. Not only that, they are constantly being amended and changed. Some follow one general model, some another, and some blend provisions of several. There are innumerable combinations and permutations of their characteristics already in existence and I am sure more to come.

There is, of course, no one perfect, all-purpose social security system, equally well suited to the needs of capitalist countries, communist countries, unitary governments, or federal-state systems. Although I have been a student of social security for over 35 years, I do not know what a social security system for all times and all places would be.

One of the fascinations of studying social security is discovering just how variable the financing of social security, the level of benefits, and the conditions of eligibility can be. Some of the factors affecting them are very apparent, some are more subtle, some almost impossible to quantify or comprehend. Historical background, economic and political institutions and beliefs, attitudes toward incentives, thrift, work, leisure, health, retirement, life expectancy, children, parents, family and the future—all of these factors play a part in determining what kind of a social security program a nation wants or accepts.

I do not believe, therefore, that our present social security system is the last word, nor do I believe it should be immune to change. On the contrary, I believe it can, it should, and it will change and that each generation should be free to remake and remold it to its needs and liking. At the same time, I recognize that there are practical limitations to such a policy. Major social institutions cannot be changed every day or even every decade—although perhaps, as Thomas Jefferson said, they might well be changed every 50 years or so. In that case, we have about 15 years to go on our present social security system and we can use the intervening years to discuss possible alternatives.

One of the key elements in social security is being able to count on what you are going to get. Of course, there is no absolutely sure thing in this world except for death and taxes. But, insofar as possible, a main goal of social security has been to give the individual citizen assurance that, come what might, he would get what was promised him, whatever this might be.

A second major goal of social security has been to divorce the payment from any need or means test and from any test of relatives' responsibility or other moral criterion. This has brought into being the concept of the payment as a matter of right—a moral, political and statutory right similar (but not identical) to the contractual right of payment under private insurance policies. Again, while we may discover there are no absolute rights, even with respect to private contracts, the effort is to make the right to social security as certain as it can be in an uncertain world.

In social security, several methods have been used to further these ends. First, the requirement that both employee and employer contribute to the program has given political, psychological and legal reality to the right. Second, the spelling out of the right in a statute has limited the discretion of the politician and administrator. Third, the fact that the individual has a statutory right to appeal through both the administrative hierarchy and the courts makes it likely that the right will be honored.

II

The need for some general governmental system of old age payments is worldwide. In 1940, 33 countries had some kind of old age program. The number increased to 44 in 1949, to 58 in 1958, and to 97 in 1969. In interpreting this substantial increase in the number of old age programs, it should be borne in mind that a total of 55 new nations received their independence between 1949 and 1969. Since there are more than 130 countries in the world today, it is clear that some governments still do not have old age programs. But those that do include all of the major industrial nations of the world, and I venture to suggest that those that do not now have some kind of governmental old age system will adopt one as their population ages.

Table I presents the main characteristics of the programs in ten countries selected to show some variations in approach. The term "tripartite" is used to mean employee, employer, and government contributions. The proportions contributed by each vary in different countries and, therefore, the use of this term should not be interpreted to mean "equal thirds." In some cases the government contributions are derived from earmarked taxes. Thus, our neighbor, Canada, has a system which differs from ours in that part of the government contribution to financing comes from a special earmarked corporate income and a manufacturer's sales tax, in addition to a personal income tax.

It is interesting that there has been a tendency in recent years to relate variable benefits to earnings in most countries instead of paying uniform benefits as was more common in the earlier part of this century. The earlier period was marked by the expectation of stable economies, very modest economic growth, and very modest rises in prices. When Sir William Beveridge was persuaded in 1942 to drop exclusive reliance on the uniform benefit in Great Britain, it was because he recognized, as an economist, the probability that postwar economies would be marked by instability, more

SUMMARY OF OLD AGE PROGRAMS IN
TEN MAJOR COUNTRIES, 1969

Country	Sources of Financing	Type of Benefits
Canada	Tripartite	Uniform plus supplement based on uniform percentage of earnings
China Nationalist	Tripartite	Lump-sum based on percentage of earnings times years of service
China Communist	Employer only	Three uniform percentages of earnings in relation to years of work
Denmark	Tripartite	Uniform plus supplement based on income
France	Tripartite	Uniform percentage of earnings
Federal Republic of Germany	Tripartite	Uniform percentage of earnings times years of coverage
Israel	Tripartite	Uniform plus supplement of uniform percentage based on years of coverage plus supplement based on income
United Kingdom	Tripartite	Uniform plus graduated plus supplementary benefits based on income
U.S.S.R.	Employer and government (no employee contribution)	Graduated
U.S.A.	Employer and employee; federal and state governments	Graduated, based on income and assets

Source: U.S. Department of Health, Education and Welfare, *Social Security Programs Throughout the World* (Washington, D.C.: Social Security Administration, 1969).

rapid economic growth due to technology and science, increased earnings, and substantial increases in prices, wages, and incomes, with little likelihood that the substantial variation in wages and incomes would diminish.

At present, only three countries in the world rely solely on universal, uniform pension plans: Finland, Iceland and New Zealand. Four other countries have such plans, but with a supplemental graduated or variable benefit superimposed on the universal basic amount: Canada, Denmark, Norway, and Sweden. All of these seven countries, with the exception of Canada, are small and homogenous with strong egalitarian and Socialist parties.

III

Although the modern type of social insurance system began some 45 years before the United States established its program in 1935, the term social security, which is now used widely throughout the world, originated in the United States. Undoubtedly, the term has become so popular because it is so general that it defies exact definition and can be accepted in vastly different societies, economies, times, and places. It expresses, at the same time, a program, an aspiration, and an evolving complex of social institutions and attitudes.

Now a curious development should be reported. The social security program of 1935 was a highly incentive-motivated program. It made employees contribute toward their benefits. It made employers contribute toward the benefits of employees. It provided differerential benefits in relation to differential earnings. It emphasized reward for work, earnings, and productivity. It was not a plan worked out by the Socialist party to redistribute income or by the Communist party to equalize wealth. It was not a program worked out by the Republican party to save the capitalistic system. It was a plan proposed by the political leaders of a party that had long emphasized states rights—leaders who established a federally operated system to save the states from bankruptcy due to the mounting number of aged who would have had to apply for state-local old age assistance at a time when the states and localities could not meet the need. It was the first of a series of federal revenue sharing plans.

By all rights, the 1935 act should have been proposed by the Republicans. Then the Democrats would have been the ones to make Alf Landon's famous Milwaukee speech of September 27, 1936, in which he called the social security program "a cruel hoax" and advocated the substitution of a uniform payment out of general revenues. The defeat of Alf Landon in 1936 prevented this alternative from being tried or even seriously considered. When, in 1953, Representative Carl Curtis tried to reopen the question with the inauguration of the first Republican administration since the Social Security Act was enacted, he was rebuffed by Secretary of Health, Education, and Welfare Oveta Culp Hobby (the first person to hold that office), Undersecretary

Nelson Rockefeller and Undersecretary of the Treasury Marion Folsom who persuaded President Eisenhower that a contributory wage-related system was more in keeping with an incentive-based enterprise economy than a uniform payment financed out of general revenues. Mrs. Hobby, an owner of a business, Mr. Folsom, a former businessman, and Mr. Rockefeller could certainly present good credentials as supporters of a free, competitive economy and a capitalistic system.

In general, the several approaches to dealing with the income problems of older people over long periods of time have been along the following lines:

The family approach. Have enough children to provide care for the parent's old age. The Chinese and other cultures tried this, but it is inconsistent with contemporary population policies.

The community approach. Take care of any dependent persons through an old people's home. This seems to be of limited interest in terms of present-day attitudes.

The individual responsibility approach. Allow each individual to arrange for his own protection through individual savings, including home ownership, asset accumulation, private insurance, pensions, and employment. This is good but it does not seem to meet everyone's needs and capacities.

Employer responsibility. Continued support by the employer in old age and employer-organized pension plans. Not everyone has an employer, and not every employer has such a plan.

The self-help approach. Union assessment plans or burial funds. They have a poor financial record.

Compulsory individual savings approach. Utilized in some small and undeveloped countries. Sometimes referred to as the Provident Fund approach, this has been of only limited value.

The welfare approach. Payment to needy persons on the basis of need. This approach was utilized on a local and state basis in the United States between 1920 and 1935 and was universalized in all states and localities by the Social Security Act of 1935. The general attitude of most Americans is a desire to avoid the welfare approach.

In 1934-35, none of these seven approaches individually or collectively was deemed entirely satisfactory to meet the growing economic and political problem of old age dependency. Hence, consideration was given to some more general plan which would deal with the problem. Four broad alternatives emerged:

1. A uniform payment to all aged persons (perhaps $30 or $40 a month) financed out of the general revenues of the federal government.

2. A federal contributory wage-related plan with variable benefits (from $10 to $85 a month) based on earnings and financed by employer and employee contributions.

3. A federal or state income-related program ("Welfare") financed out of general revenues and payable to

all needy persons with income and assets below a given level.

4. Some other program or programs along with the plan selected, such as a voluntary or compulsory saving or annuity program.

The 1935 decision was to accept plan (2) as the longer-run goal, coupled with a welfare plan (3) for those who were not adequately covered by the social security plan. The hope was that the welfare portion for the aged would ultimately wither away.

IV

In assessing private and public responsibilities for old age support, the following guidelines seem to me the "conventional wisdom" of the present:

1. Both public and private means should be utilized in dealing with the financial needs of the old. It is not desirable to rely on one method exclusively. Nor has it been found feasible.

2. Any program should provide incentives for the individual to save and accumulate additional income.

3. Individuals should have the freedom to work or not to work after the normal retirement age, especially to work part-time. Those who continue to work should receive a somewhat higher benefit when they retire.

4. One objective of a government social security program should be to eliminate poverty among the aged. But, in an incentive economy, this should not be its sole objective.

5. The smaller the number of aged persons receiving an income-related payment, the better. The proportion of the aged who have to receive such a payment should, in my opinion, not exceed one percent. (That would be about 200,000 at the present time.)

6. Any government program should be administered by the federal government so that all persons in similar circumstances throughout the nation would be treated similarly.

7. Employers, unions and individuals should be encouraged to contribute to private pension plans with the government granting appropriate tax advantages and setting standards to ensure some vesting of benefits, portability, reinsurance and security of funds.

8. Any general government program should provide some individual and employer responsibility for financing. The exact proportions for each might vary in relation to many factors, such as contributions to other programs, the age of retirement, the impact of taxes on the economy and other considerations.

I oppose at this time any proposal to substitute for the present system, in whole or in part, a system of uniform payments to every aged person either without regard to income or taking income into account. Such a system is easily susceptible to political and emotional manipulation. For instance, if the uniform payment were $100 a month, it would be easy to rally political support for an increase to $150 a month, or $200 a month or some higher figure. Certainly, all definite amounts in any legislation are subject to pressures for increase. But a uniform payment, which assumes that the costs will be financed out of general revenues (or an earmarked income tax), is particularly susceptible to pressures for increases and, in periods of budgetary constraints or economic stress, to pressures for decreases and for various restrictions relating to assets and other eligibility conditions.

I also oppose any wholesale substitute for the social security system, whatever its name (such as a negative income tax, a guaranteed income or what have you) that makes payments only to the poor. A program for the poor will most likely be a poor program.

My own opinion is that the *minimum* social security benefit should be set at approximately the poverty level (established according to the general conceptual assumptions of the present poverty yardsticks). This level, at 1970 prices, would be approximately $150 a month for a single person and $200 to $225 for a couple. But, above the minimum, benefits should have some relation to earnings. The variation between the minimum and maximum should be great enough to ensure psychological as well as financial support from a majority of taxpayers and beneficiaries.

Benefits should be adjusted from time to time to reflect changes in prices. But I do not believe that mere adjustments for price changes are an adequate old age security policy for a dynamic, incentive, democratic economy.

I believe that a major public policy question is how the aged (and the disabled, widows and orphans) can share appropriately in the total productivity and affluence of the nation. More specifically, as productivity, earnings and income increase for the nation as a whole, how can these improvements be reflected among those in our society who are not primarily in the labor force? The wage-price-profit system tends to allocate rewards primarily to persons in the labor force and their immediate dependents. Thus, by itself, this system is not a satisfactory mechanism to handle rewards to, say, widows over 75 who have never been in the paid labor force or whose husbands left the labor force ten or fifteen years previously or who have no children. Neither the market nor the family, separately or together, can today handle the problem of old age security without governmental intervention. The only question today, in my opinion, is the nature of the governmental intervention.

The fact of the matter is that the overwhelming majority of the business and union leaders at the present time accept the basic premises of the present graduated government social security system. So do the major political leaders. Support for radical departures such as the Townsend plan on the one hand or a voluntary social security system on the other is quite limited. Any plan involving millions of persons and billions of dollars must have the support of millions of persons.

There are several other important questions still being

debated in relation to the existing program. Some of the major ones are:

1. To what extent is there a limit to payroll taxes as a basis for financing social security? Should general revenues be utilized? If so, on what basis and to what extent?

2. Should low income persons be exempt, in part or whole, from the payroll tax?

3. To what extent should the maximum earnings basis (now $7,800 a year) on which contributions and benefits are computed be increased?

4. What is the appropriate normal retirement age? Should actuarial reductions at earlier ages be provided?

5. What is the level of benefits (minimum, maximum) that should be paid to aged persons and on what basis should they be paid?

6. What changes should be made in the "retirement test" (now $1,680 a year plus a 50 percent offset on the next $1,200 and an annuity payable at age 72 without regard to retirement)?

Some of these questions might be answered differently depending upon the answers to one particular question. For instance, if the normal retirement age (at which full-rate benefits are payable) were 55 or 75, the answer to the question on benefit levels might be different. If the range in benefits from the minimum to the maximum were 1-to-2 instead of 1-to-4 as at present, the answer to the question on financing might be different.

I would also modify my answers somewhat depending on the availability of health care and its costs after retirement. Thus, if a reasonably complete health insurance program were available to all aged persons with little or no costs after retirement, this should be taken into account in determining the level of benefits.

I speak for the view that the nation should be generous toward the elderly. Generous, not only for humanitarian and ethical reasons, but because it is sound economics and intelligent politics.

The maintenance, development and dynamism of our economic system depend upon the willingness of individuals to work conscientiously, to take risks, and to innovate. And individuals should know that, at the completion of their normal years of work, there will be a reasonably adequate assurance of income and health protection for them whether or not they have been successful every time in taking risks, in trying to do something new or different.

Social security is a form of income guarantee for the aged, the disabled, the widow and orphan. As a nation we are committed to that principle for these groups. The question of how much, the conditions under which the benefits are to be paid, and how they are to be financed are important, debatable and subject to change.

If a basic uniform payment to all persons or to all the aged in the United States were to be enacted which took *income into account,* I do not see how that should modify the social security system. If a uniform payment to the aged were to be paid *without regard to income,* then I would propose that the social security program be revised to make it into a "double-decker" system, but with a variable second deck which would be consistent with an economy which recognizes variations in income, standards of living and rewards.

The proposal recommended in early 1971 by the Committee on Ways and Means of the House of Representatives involves the following "holy trinity":

1. Utilizing the contributory, earnings-related variable benefit approach under OASDI to provide the basic floor of protection, with employer and employee financing and a moderate trust fund to handle short-term fluctuations, errors and contingencies without having to resort to emergency financing or dependence on the general revenues of government. Benefits would not be based on the assets of the individual or income derived from such assets.

2. A minimum income guarantee to the needy aged (and the blind and disabled) based on income and assets.

3. Utilizing private pensions, savings, home ownership, family and community resources as a supplement to the two nationwide plans.

This pluralistic system has been designed to try to give weight to both social responsibility and individual responsibility, retaining incentives to work and save, and permitting the adjustment of levels of total income to varying concepts. It is certainly not the only way to meet these objectives and certainly not the final answer. But it is a reasonably good approach for this economy, and one which is susceptible to incremental improvements over time as our productivity and gross national product increase.

I suspect that over the next thirty years or so our ideas about work, leisure, retirement, and income will be changing. Let us assume that, in 1995, the normal retirement age is 55, the normal workweek is 30 hours, the normal vacation period per year is six weeks, that life expectancy at birth is closer to 75 years than the present 70, that per capita income at present prices is 50 percent higher than today, and that 75 percent of all women are working 20 hours a week for pay. In that situation, I think we might have a different old age security system than we have now.

But I think it more appropriate for my children and grandchildren to grapple with that problem then than for us to try to anticipate it now.

SECOND LECTURE

MILTON FRIEDMAN

The Great Depression and the subsequent New Deal reforms produced many governmental programs designed to mitigate poverty and indigence. This paper is concerned with the two such programs—social security and public assistance—that have involved far and away the largest amount of governmental expenditures. The breeding ground for both programs was the widespread unemployment and hardship that reached its zenith in 1933 but continued at a high level throughout the rest of the '30s.

Social security was intended as a permanent program to enable working people to provide for their own retirement and for temporary periods of unemployment and thus avoid becoming objects of charity. Public assistance was intended as a temporary program for persons in distress, to be largely phased out as employment improved and as social security matured. Both programs started small. Both have grown like Topsy. There is no sign that social security has displaced assistance—both are at all time highs in terms of dollar

---

I am greatly indebted to Rosemary and Colin Campbell for constructive and critical comments on earlier drafts and for preparing the basic data presented in the appendix to this lecture.

expenditures and of number of persons receiving payments. In 1970, social security "benefits" of $43 billion were paid to more than 36 million recipients.[1] Public assistance payments of nearly $14.5 billion were made to well over 13 million recipients.

The question now is: where do we go from here? Widespread dissatisfaction with the public assistance program—with the so-called welfare mess—has produced numerous proposals for drastic reform, including the President's proposed Family Assistance Plan now before the Congress. On the other hand, general complacency about social security is reflected in pressure to expand it still farther.

My own attitude toward the two programs is almost the reverse. Bad as the welfare mess is, at least public assistance does go mainly to needy persons who are at lower income levels than the persons paying the taxes to finance the payments. The system badly needs reform but, at the moment, it serves an essential social function. It seems impossible to eliminate it promptly, even though its elimination should be our long-term objective. On the other hand, social security [2] combines a highly regressive tax with largely indiscriminate benefits and, in overall effect, probably redistributes income from lower to higher income persons. I believe that it serves no essential social function. Existing commitments make it impossible to eliminate it overnight, but it should be unwound and terminated as soon as possible.

Reform welfare; unwind social security; and, in the

process, construct a system that will do efficiently and humanely what our present welfare and social security system does inefficiently and inhumanely—namely, provide an assured minimum to all persons in need regardless of the reason for their need without destroying their character, their independence, or their incentive to better their own conditions. In developing this thesis, I shall consider, first, social security retirement and survivors' benefits; then, briefly, the welfare system; then a program for reform.

I. Retirement Benefits

A widely distributed, unsigned HEW booklet entitled "Your Social Security" begins:

> The basic idea of social security is a simple one: During working years employees, their employers, and self-employed people pay social security contributions which are pooled in special trust funds. When earnings stop or are reduced because the worker retires, dies, or becomes disabled, monthly cash benefits are paid to replace part of the earnings the family has lost.

This is Orwellian doublethink.

—Payroll taxes are labelled "contributions" (or, as the Party might have put it in the book *1984*, "Compulsory is Voluntary").

—Trust funds are conjured with as if they played an important role when, in fact, they are extremely small ($32.5 billion for OASI as of December 1970) and consist simply of promises by one branch of the government to pay another branch. Over a decade ago, the Social Security Administration estimated that the present value of the old age pensions already promised to persons covered by social security (both those who had retired and those who had not) was over $300 billion. The corresponding sum must be far larger today. That is the size of the trust fund that would be required to justify the words of the booklet. ("Little is Much.")

—The impression is given that a worker's "benefits" are financed by his "contributions." The fact is that taxes currently being collected from current workers are being used to pay benefits to persons who have retired or to their dependents and survivors. No trust fund in any meaningful sense is being accumulated. ("I am You.")

A worker paying taxes today can derive no assurance from trust funds that he will receive benefits when he retires. Any assurance derives solely from the willingness of future taxpayers to impose taxes on themselves to finance benefits being promised by present taxpayers to ourselves. This one-sided "compact between the generations," foisted on generations that literally cannot give their consent, may be sufficient assurance, but it certainly is a very different thing from a "trust fund." A chain letter would be a more accurate designation.

The HEW booklet goes on to say, "Nine out of ten working people in the United States are now building protection for themselves and their families under the social security system."

More doublethink. What nine out of ten working people are now doing is paying taxes to finance payments to persons who are not working. The individual worker is in no sense building protection for himself and his family—as a person who contributes to a private vested pension system is building his own protection. Persons who are now receiving payments are receiving much more than the actuarial value of the taxes that they paid and that were paid on their behalf. Young persons who are now paying social security taxes are being promised much less than the actuarial value of the taxes that they paid and that were paid on their behalf.

More fundamentally yet, "the relationship between individual contributions (that is, payroll taxes) and benefits received is extremely tenuous." [3] Millions of people who pay taxes will never receive any benefits attributable to those taxes because they will not have paid for enough quarters to qualify, or because they receive payments in their capacity as spouse. Persons who pay vastly different sums over their working lives may receive identically the same benefits. Two men or two women who pay precisely the same taxes at the same time may end up receiving different benefits because one is married and the other is single. A man who continues working after age 65 will be required to pay additional taxes, and yet may receive no benefits at all. This list can be extended indefinitely.

The fact is that social security is not in any meaningful sense an insurance program in which individual payments purchase equivalent actuarial benefits. It is a combination of a particular tax—a flat rate tax on wages up to a maximum—and a particular program of transfer payments, in which all sorts of considerations other than the amount paid determine the amount received.

I have long been fascinated that hardly anyone approves of either part separately. Yet the two combined have become a sacred cow. What a triumph of imaginative packaging and Madison Avenue advertising!

I have dwelt on the difference between rhetoric and reality because the smoke screen laid down by advocates of expanded social security has made it difficult to see clearly the key issues. This smoke screen must be penetrated, and revealed for what it is, if we are ever to make our way out of the morass that social security has become, and avoid the even greater problems that lie ahead.

As I have gone through the literature, I have been shocked at the level of the arguments that have been used to sell social security, not only by politicians or special-interest groups, but more especially by self-righteous academics. Men who would not lie to their children, their friends, or their colleagues, whom you and I would trust implicitly in personal dealings, have propagated a false view of social security—and their intelligence and exposure to contrary views make it hard to believe that they have done so unintentionally and innocently. The very name—old age and survivors insurance—is a blatant attempt to mislead the public into identifying a compulsory tax and benefit system with private, voluntary, and individual purchase of individually assured benefits. What am I to make of professors at leading institutions, of high-level bureaucrats, of cabinet and sub-cabinet officials who compare the future benefits promised to young workers solely with the tax nominally levied on employees, often not even mentioning that they are completely excluding the equivalent tax levied on employers? They know very well that common sense, economic theory, and empirical evidence all support the view that the distinction between the social security tax paid directly by the employee and the tax paid by the employer is primarily the label attached to components of the employers' cost of labor.[4] Both are proportional to wage rates; both enter labor costs; both are borne equally by the employee.[5] Perhaps a tortured argument can be made that the employee and employer taxes have somewhat different effects but surely no one can maintain that no part of the tax paid by the employer is to be assimilated to the tax paid by the employee.

Or, again, what am I to make of such high-minded gentlemen protesting in one breath the accuracy of the insurance terminology and objecting in the next to full payment of benefits to persons between 65 and 72 who continue to work on the ground that the "need" of these elders is less than that of other persons to whom the money could be paid. If, indeed, the benefits are linked to "contributions," the need argument is irrelevant. If the criterion of need is relevant, then the talk about "insurance," about benefits linked to "contributions," is simply hogwash.

Let us then disassemble the misleading package and look at the tax part and the benefit part separately— restricting ourselves to the old age and survivors program alone, but noting incidentally that the discussion is in the main equally relevant to the disability, health, and unemployment programs. Having looked at each part separately, I shall digress to consider the recent ingenious "compact between the generations" argument.

Social security tax

The social security tax is a flat rate tax on covered earnings up to a maximum. The rate on wages and salaries is half paid directly by employees, half paid by employers on behalf of their employees. A lower rate is imposed on earnings of self-employed persons. Wages paid to persons not covered, or earnings of self-employed not covered, are not subject to tax.

Currently (early 1971), the rate of OASI alone is 8.1 percent split between employers and employees, and 6.075 percent on the earnings of the self-employed, in both cases up to maximum earnings of $7,800. The rate for OASDHI (old age, survivors, disability, and hospital insurance) is 10.4 percent on wages and 7.5 percent on the earnings of the self-employed, and there is an additional tax for unemployment insurance. Coverage is by now nearly universal.

What can we say about this tax viewed solely as a tax?

1. These are very heavy taxes on very low incomes. For most persons with incomes less than the maximum covered, the social security tax is many times larger than the personal income tax.

2. The tax is regressive because of the maximum limit and the absence of an exemption.

3. It is hard to see any excuse for the differential between the rates on wages and salaries and on earnings from self-employment. The differential is mitigated, but probably only a trifle, by the fact that none of the tax on self-employment is deductible in computing the federal personal income tax while half the tax on wages is not included in the wages reported for tax purposes. Presumably, the heavier tax on the hired worker than on the self-employed worker is the price in equity that has been paid to preserve the fiction that the employer tax is not borne by the employee!

4. The exclusion of earnings from uncovered employment is unjustifiable from the tax point of view, but this is now trivial.

5. No allowance at all is made for family size.

6. The tax is solely on realized income from personal services. All property income is excluded, along, of course, with imputed income from services. This item is important because it means that the tax is an incentive to obtain income in other forms—in nonmarket

forms such as leisure, or do-it-yourself activities, from relief and public assistance instead of work, and from property instead of work.

7. The tax rate is raised drastically for persons between 65 and 72 who are eligible for benefits, choose to work, and earn more than $140 a month. The marginal social security tax rate on earnings from $140 a month to $240 a month is 60.4 percent, and from $240 a month until benefits are reduced to zero, 110.4 percent. When the unemployment taxes and federal, state and local taxes are included, the overall marginal rates are still higher. Little wonder that there has been a sharp decline in recent years in the fraction of persons in this age group who work as more of them have become eligible for social security payments.

8. The tax has risen very rapidly. Tax receipts for OASI alone have risen more than 11-fold from 1950 to 1970, and the average tax paid per covered person, by over 7.5-fold. The maximum tax payable on behalf of an employee has risen from $90 in 1950 to $632 in 1971, or by 7-fold, and this understates the rise because there should be added to this sum the federal income tax paid on account of the payroll tax levied directly on the employee, which undoubtedly has risen even more sharply.

In summary: the payroll tax is almost surely far and away the most regressive element in our tax system and a significant disincentive to work. Discussions of the incentive effects of taxes have generally emphasized the disincentive effects of high marginal rates on high incomes. It may well be that the high marginal rates on low incomes have become an equally serious disincentive.

Relation of tax to benefits

The justification given for so regressive a tax has always been that taxes are linked to benefits. Though this justification has some validity, it mitigates the deficiencies of the tax only to a very minor extent.

The valid key elements are:

1. Benefits are paid (with one minor exception) only to persons who have paid taxes.[6]

2. The size of the benefit is related to the average wage on which taxes were levied, rising with that wage rate.

3. There is an absolute maximum to the benefit paid, justifying an absolute maximum to the tax paid.

These points provide some basis for regarding the tax as a price paid for a benefit. Generally, the price paid for identical goods and services is the same regardless of the income of the purchaser.

The limitations of this justification are severe:

1. Most important of all, tax payments are compulsory. The wage earner cannot decide whether he wishes to purchase the benefit, or what size benefit he wishes to purchase.

2. Many people who pay taxes receive no benefits at all. Insofar as this occurs because they die before

retirement, this may be regarded as appropriate: they have simply bought an actuarial right and have had the bad luck to die before they could realize on it. But it also occurs for reasons that violate the concept of purchase. Persons who do not pay taxes for enough quarters to qualify get nothing whatsoever for their payments. Many others who do qualify get nothing because they are entitled to higher benefits by virtue of their spouse's eligibility. (A retired wife who is age 65 or over at claim is entitled to one-half her husband's benefit. A widow who is age 62 or over at claim gets 82½ percent of her late husband's benefit. A wife or a widow cannot receive *both* the benefit based on her earnings and the benefit she is entitled to as a wife, or a widow.)

3. That part of the variation in the benefit that is related to average wages refers only to average wages for part of the working career. More important, it varies much less than in proportion to wages. Currently, the maximum wage-related benefit is about three times the minimum; but the maximum "average monthly wage" on which benefits are based can, for persons retiring in 1971, be over 80 times the minimum sufficient to qualify.[7]

4. Taxes paid vary even more widely than "average monthly wage" because of variation in the number of years for which taxes were paid and in wages received in years not counted in computing the "average monthly wage." The benefit varies widely for reasons having

SECOND LECTURE   33

nothing whatsoever to do with taxes paid, namely, marital status and number of dependents.

5. From 1950 to 1971, the maximum tax payable on behalf of an employee rose 7-fold. From 1950 to 1970, the average tax paid per covered person rose over 7.5-fold. The maximum benefit eventually receivable, on the other hand, rose 3.5-fold; the maximum benefit currently receivable, a trifle over 3-fold; the average monthly benefit actually paid, less than 3-fold, and the minimum benefit 3.5-fold. However one looks at it, taxes have risen roughly two times more than benefits.

These points explain why Pechman, Aaron, and Taussig, who start their book by asserting that "the social security system is among the most effective and successful institutions ever developed in the United States," nonetheless say, as already quoted, "the relationship between individual contributions (that is, payroll taxes) and benefits received is extremely tenuous." [8] If you wish to predict how much a person is now receiving as a benefit or is likely to receive when he retires, you will do far better to ask what is his sex, marital status, and age than to ask how much he did pay or will pay in taxes.

The minor linkage between payments and benefits is a smoke screen, not a valid justification for so imperfect a tax. Yet the emphasis that has been given to the smoke screen makes it worth asking which groups have received or are likely to receive the highest benefits relative to taxes paid and which the lowest. That is, if we do view the system as linking taxes and benefits, who is getting a bargain and who is being taken? The complexity and looseness of the relation between taxes and benefits make it difficult to answer this question unambiguously and comprehensively, but a few points are clear.

1. The major distinction is age. The older persons were blanketed into the system, paid taxes for only part of their working life, and even then at low rates. Up to date, probably almost all persons who have retired—except only for those who continued working between ages 65 and 72—have received an actuarial value much larger than the accumulated value of the taxes they paid. This fact, of course, helps to explain both the more rapid rise in taxes than in benefits and the popularity of the system among older citizens.

Younger persons are, under present law, being promised benefits much lower than the actuarial value of the taxes being paid on their behalf.[9]

2. A second key distinction is the date at which a group was covered. Those blanketed in last have been required to pay taxes for the fewest years. This group includes self-employed and professional groups, university professors and employees of other nonprofit institutions, and farm and domestic workers. So it includes both relatively high and relatively low income groups.

3. A related category consists of persons in the still uncovered areas, mostly governmental employees who have separate pension funds. With moonlighting, early

retirement, or a working wife, they can easily qualify for the minimum social security benefit—which, as we have seen, is extremely generous compared to the minimum taxes that must be paid to qualify—in addition to their other federal or state government pension.

4. If we consider the system in full operation and neglect the starting up problems, it then seems clear that persons in high income classes will receive higher benefits relative to taxes paid than persons in low income classes.

a) Persons in high income classes typically start working at a later age and so will tend to pay taxes for a shorter period.

b) Persons in high income classes have a higher life expectancy, and so will tend to receive benefits for a longer period.

c) The employer tax is excluded from the personal tax base, which is of much greater advantage to persons in high income classes.

d) Even more important, the social security benefit is not subject to the personal income tax, which again is a greater advantage to persons in high income classes.

e) The self-employed pay a lower tax rate, and while some are in low income groups, many, particularly professionals, are in high income groups.

The only counterweight to all this is the fact that benefits vary to a modest degree with the "average monthly wage," and even this advantage to persons in lower income groups may well be offset by the greater likelihood that such persons will be employed in covered industry for too few quarters to qualify for benefits.

5. Single persons receive lower benefits than married persons, though this is offset by the fact that a married woman receives *either* the benefit based on her earnings or her benefit as a wife.

Benefit structure

The tenuous relation between taxes and benefits makes it desirable to look at the benefit structure taken by itself. From this point of view, it falls between two stools. It gives too much attention to "need" to be justified as return for taxes paid, and it gives too much attention to taxes paid to be justified as adequately linked to need.

1. Some persons are excluded entirely because they are not covered.

2. Eligibility for benefits is not related to current income or to current assets, except for the link to earnings of persons between 65 and 72. As a result, most social security payments go to persons who would not be regarded as entitled to benefits on the basis of the kind of "need" criterion that is embodied in public assistance programs or that would be embodied in a satisfactory negative income tax.

3. Differences in benefits paid are not related to "need" in a clear and satisfactory way. Differences in need do not explain differences in benefits related to past earnings, or differences in benefits paid the primary

recipient and a surviving spouse. The variation in payments by family size has been criticized as inappropriate.[10]

4. Benefits are not adjusted to inflation, in a dual sense. First, average earnings determining the size of benefits are not adjusted for price changes during the working lifetime. Second, benefits are adjusted for inflation during retirement only by occasional congressionally enacted changes in benefits. This defect is common to most public assistance programs.

In short, viewed as a way to distribute government assistance to the needy, the structure of benefits is not defensible and is not defended even by the proponents of social security. Insofar as they defend it at all, they do so by adding to the objective of assisting the needy, the objective of protecting "individuals from severe declines in living standards in retirement" [11]—needless to say, whether they want to be protected or not!

Compact between the generations

As the insurance analogy has worn thin, a new rationalization for social security has been developed, namely, that it "should be regarded as an institutionalized compact between the working and nonworking generations." Granted that "in return for his own contribution to the social security funds, an individual does not earn a *quid pro quo* in the private insurance sense, he does earn a *quid pro quo* in a sense that is, perhaps, even more fundamental. Since he gives up part of his earnings during his own working life to support the aged during their retirement, he has a strong moral claim to similar support from future working-age generations during his own retirement. Although the benefits are earned rights, and in this sense may be accorded protection under procedural due process, they are not accorded the property protection which funded premium rights would be given. The only assurance that benefits will continue to be paid is Congressional unwillingness to repeal the program." [12]

This approach has the great appeal that it explains how every generation may be able to get greater benefits than would be justified on an actuarial basis by the taxes it pays. Given a growing population and rising per capita wages, taxes yielded by a fixed percentage rate on wages up to a maximum of currently employed workers and used to pay current benefits will be spread among a smaller number of workers who paid their taxes on lower wages. Hence the apparent paradox: each generation can get more than it paid—so long as the growth continues and the new generations play the game.

These arguments are generally cited *as if* they justified compulsory social security of the existing kind. However, they do not do so, in a dual sense.

First and less fundamental, suppose these arguments justified subsidization of retirement benefits from tax funds. Such subsidization could readily be accomplished without nationalization of the industry of providing retirement benefits, as James Buchanan has demonstrated.[13]

Second and more fundamental, morality is, to my view, an individual matter, not a class matter. Insofar as there is an implicit "compact between generations," is it not the compact embodied in the Ten Commandments: "Honor thy father and thy mother"? Does it not call for *individuals* to give of their free will of their current substance to assist the elderly (and others in need) who in their day did likewise? And does not the chain-letter argument enhance the ability of individuals and not merely classes to support earlier generations?

It takes an implicit Marxian class interpretation—antithetical I believe to the fundamental ethics of Western civilization—to convert this argument for individual responsibility into an argument for the responsibility of one class (the present generation) to another class (the earlier generation), and into an argument for a compulsory tax on the present generation to provide governmental subsidies to an earlier generation. Hopefully, we can transmit a tradition of moral responsibility to our children. If we succeed, we need not try to impose a legal responsibility on them. If we fail, we shall not be able to impose a legal responsibility on them.

Indeed, is there not something immoral in our making promises to ourselves that can be redeemed only by our children? I grant at once that this is a complex issue and cannot be answered in ringing tones. The continuation of civilization requires many measures that can succeed only with the compliance of future generations. But should we not minimize rather than enlarge such compacts between generations?

I submit that the argument based on a "compact between the generations" is no less a smoke screen than the insurance analogy.

Conclusion regarding social security

My conclusion is that the present system cannot be justified. We stumbled into it because of the special problems raised by the Great Depression. That depression was produced by government mismanagement of the monetary system, yet paradoxically became the justification for further extension of governmental controls. Massive unemployment and widespread hardship to both young and old produced by bad monetary policy were interpreted as demonstrating that individuals could not or would not themselves provide for their old age or for other vicissitudes of life and that government had to force them to do so or do so for them. And once adopted, like most government programs, social security accumulated vested interests and grew and grew and grew until, today, a program that was intended as a supplementary program to keep the aged off the relief rolls collects taxes each year (for OASDHI) roughly equal to the whole of personal savings.

It was a mistake, I believe, to have enacted social security in the first place. But having done so, we cannot abolish it overnight. We have entered into com-

mitments with millions of persons that should be ful-
filled. And these commitments are for a long period,
so total unwinding will take a long time. However,
our goal should be to eliminate the payroll tax completely, to end the present complex structure of benefits
and entitlements, to get the government out of the
pseudo-pension business, and to combine the valid elements in the benefit structure with a single comprehensive program of assistance to the indigent.

Before outlining a specific program for achieving
these objectives, I shall discuss briefly public assistance,
since a satisfactory program of reform should encompass
both.

II. Public Assistance

I can be far briefer in discussing the "welfare mess"
than in discussing social security for on this question
I am, at long last, swimming with the tide and not
against it. The defects of our present system of welfare
have become widely recognized: growing numbers on
welfare despite growing prosperity; a vast bureaucracy
largely devoted to shuffling papers rather than to serv-
ing people; the demeaning character of relief; the
difficulty of persons on relief getting off of it, thereby
creating two classes of citizens; the other side of this
coin, namely, a lack of incentive for persons on relief
to earn income; wide variation in relief payments from
one part of the country to another, encouraging migra-
tion from the South and rural areas to the North and

particularly to urban metropolises; differential treatment of persons at essentially the same economic level,
depending on whether they are or have been on relief
or have not been on relief (the so-called working poor).

The major component of public assistance, and the
rapidly growing component, is AFDC, aid to families
of dependent children. This accounts for $5 billion of
the total $9 billion of direct money payments in 1970
to recipients of public assistance and for nearly 10
million of the 14 million recipients of such payments.
The remaining $4 billion of direct money payments is
divided among old age assistance, aid to the blind, aid
to the permanently and totally disabled, general assistance, emergency assistance, and institutional service in
intermediate care facilities. In addition, nearly $6 billion
was spent under public assistance programs for hospital
and medical care.

The President's Family Assistance Plan is in principle
a far-reaching proposal for restructuring public assistance. Its aims are, first, to establish a national minimum
welfare standard, thereby reducing the incentive for
poor people to move in order to qualify for higher
welfare; second, to give persons on relief a strong
incentive to work themselves off relief by enabling them
to improve their lot substantially by additional earnings;
and third, to substitute an objective income standard
for the present means test and thereby provide more
equal treatment.

These objectives are admirable, and the general principle embodied in the proposal—a negative income tax—is well suited to achieve them. But unfortunately, the specific embodiment of these principles is so defective that the bill, at least in the form in which it was submitted to the Senate Finance Committee last year, would make matters worse rather than better. The key difficulty is that in order to avoid disturbing existing programs, the bill has been so drafted that it gives even less incentive to persons on or off relief to get off or stay off relief than they now have.[14] Perhaps the version now (carly 1971) being developed by the House Ways and Means Committee will rectify some of these defects.

One source of difficulty that is of special relevance for the present discussion is social security. Consider a person on relief who takes a job. After the first $720 of earnings a year, the President proposes that the welfare payment be reduced by 50 cents for every dollar of additional earnings, supposedly leaving the worker 50 cents for himself. However, part of the remaining 50 cents will be absorbed by the employee social security tax, which is 5.2 percent of the total wage, so the amount left will be 44.8 cents instead of 50 cents. And that is not all. The employer will not hire the worker unless the worker's product will cover his wage cost, and this includes the employer OASDHI tax and the unemployment tax, which together amount to 8.3 percent on earnings up to $3,000 a year. Accordingly, a wage cost of 108.3 cents leaves the worker with only 44.8 cents additional—a total marginal tax rate of 58.6 percent. Unfortunately, even that is not the end. Food stamp benefits, state supplements, medical care and housing benefits may also be reduced as a result of the earnings. The result is that over a wide range of earnings the actual marginal tax rate reaches 80 percent and more.

III. Proposal for Reform

I have long believed that the major defect of our present arrangements is the proliferation of special programs either for special groups or special commodities: OASDHI for some retired or disabled, old age assistance for others, unemployment insurance, aid to the blind, AFDC, food stamp plans, public housing, urban renewal, medicaid, farm subsidies, et cetera. Whatever the good intentions of the initial proponents of these programs, the programs tend to become the preserve of special vested interests and come to serve purposes very different from those that they were initially designed to serve.

The total amount of money spent on these and similar programs, federal, state, and local, exceeded $75 billion in 1969-70.[15] If this were divided among the 24.3 million persons classified as "poor" in 1969 under the arbitrary social security definition (4,950,000 families plus 4,851,000 unattached individuals), it would come to over $3,000 per person, a sum that nearly equals the average income of all persons in the United States. The problem is not that the government is spending too little on redistributive programs but that most of the money spent is not going to the poor.

The correct direction in which to move, I believe, is to replace all of these programs by a single program designed to give assistance to persons with low incomes, regardless of the reason why their incomes are low—whether because they are old or unemployed, unskilled or ill, physically or mentally handicapped, or whatever. Such a comprehensive program would cost far less each year than the present ragbag of programs. Yet it would come far closer to alleviating true distress.

The program that has long seemed to me best suited for this purpose is a negative income tax linked with the positive income tax and replacing the whole group of particular programs. There is no necessity for repeating here the advantages and disadvantages of a comprehensive positive and negative income tax, for discussing its details, or for examining problems of administration. My views on these questions have been amply spelled out elsewhere.[16] What I do want to discuss are the transitional problems insofar as these relate to our special topic, old age and survivors' benefits.

How can this program be wound down without injustice to persons now covered? My agenda is as follows:

1. Repeal the payroll tax.
2. Terminate any further accumulation of benefits.
3. Enact a negative income tax, treating payments

under social security as income for purposes of determining eligibility for benefits.

4. Continue to pay all existing beneficiaries the amounts that they are entitled to under current law, except that these amounts should automatically be escalated over time by any changes in cost of living. This will meet our commitments in real, not nominal, terms. Give such beneficiaries an option to accept a capital sum equal to the present value of the payments instead of continuing payments.

5. Give every worker who has earned coverage under present law a commitment to the retirement and survivors' benefits that he would be entitled to under present law, given his present tax payments and earnings record. This commitment would be in the form of *either* a promise to pay the specified annual sum at the future date when under present law he would be entitled to the sum *or* government bonds equal in market value to the present value of those benefits, calculated at the market interest rate on government obligations of corresponding maturity, at the option of the worker.

6. Give every worker who has had taxes paid on his behalf but has not yet earned coverage a capital sum equal to the accumulated value of the taxes that have been paid on his behalf.

7. Finance payments under 4, 5, and 6 out of general tax funds plus the issuance of government bonds.

Note that in the main these items simply recognize explicitly and fund obligations that now exist in an unfunded form. They do not add in any way to the true debt of the government but simply terminate the accumulation of any further obligations. These steps would enable the bulk of the present social security administrative apparatus to be dismantled at once. It would be necessary to keep only a declining staff to administer item 4.

Such a winding down of social security would eliminate its present disincentive effects on work, and so would mean a larger national income currently. It would add to personal saving which would mean a higher rate of capital formation and a more rapid rate of growth of income. It would stimulate the development and expansion of private pension plans and so add to the security of many workers.

I realize that this is a radical proposal that goes strongly against present trends. I have therefore searched for less radical measures that would be more acceptable in the short-run and yet lead in the right long-run direction. One proposal along these lines has been made by James Buchanan and Colin Campbell: fund the unfunded obligations, set tax rates that would correspond to benefits promised, and permit individuals to opt out of the system provided they arranged for equivalent pensions for themselves by voluntary means.[17] Such a program would be an improvement over the present system but retains the undesirable features of keeping the U.S. government in the pension business and of compelling people to distribute their income between present and future in a designated way. I have not been able to develop any other more gradual proposal that appeals as much.

In closing, it is interesting to note the degree of overlap between my agenda and that of Pechman, Aaron, and Taussig. Despite their approval of social security, despite their acceptance of the imposition by the government of a compact between the generations, their proposal for "total reform" overlaps mine completely with respect to the negative income tax and the repeal of the payroll tax. However, they would retain in addition an earnings-related retirement benefit to be financed from other taxes. Similarly, even their less radical reform proposals overlap mine in calling for the repeal of the payroll tax as an independent tax.

Social security programs involve annual expenditures of roughly $43 billion. These programs appear on balance to transfer income from relatively low income classes to middle and upper income classes. They are flourishing, are widely regarded as highly successful, and seem destined to expand.

Welfare programs involve annual expenditures of $15 billion. These programs appear on balance to transfer income from middle and upper income classes to lower income classes. They are in a state of crisis, are widely regarded as intolerable, and seem destined to be transformed.

Is this another example of Director's law in operation? Director's law of public income redistribution is as follows: "Public expenditures are made for the primary benefit of the middle class, and financed with taxes which are borne in considerable part by the poor and rich." [18]

REBUTTALS

WILBUR J. COHEN

Mr. Friedman probably makes a good point when he says that the tax and benefit aspects of the social security system, considered separately, could not be justified. But that does not mean that they are not sound when you look at them together.

My analogy would be that a man can be looked at alone, a woman can be looked at alone, but when you put them together something happens. [Laughter.] That is what has happened in social security. Putting the two elements together has created something new, and it is more than rhetoric.

Mr. Friedman also attacks the insurance aspects of social security and his criticism suggests he doesn't know what insurance is. He gives us a Friedman definition, but not the right definition.

Insurance does not mean that you have to have an actuarial relationship between the individual contributions and the individual benefits. No group insurance in the United States would qualify as insurance under his test. I won't argue about his definition. If he wants to have his definition, let him have it. It is not mine, and it is not the definition that the Congress of the

United States has given. Congress has called social security insurance. And my article in the *Encyclopaedia Britannica* calls it insurance. [Laughter.]

So take your pick. [Laughter.]

Mr. Friedman calls a lot of the things he doesn't like about social security rhetoric. And that gets me to a point I want to stress. My point is that economists do not determine all of the choices and options and attitudes prevailing in this nation. People do live by rhetoric. You can't understand what goes on in the United States if you don't understand something about rhetoric. And think of all the people in this audience who would be out of a job if we didn't have such a thing as rhetoric. [Laughter.]

I believe in rhetoric because it makes a lot of things palatable that might be unpalatable to economists. [Laughter.]

Finally, Mr. Friedman attacks the idea that American social security is primarily a system of redistribution of income to middle income people. Actually I think he is probably right about that. But, that is part of the system's political sagacity. Since most of the people in the United States are in the middle income, middle class range, social security is a program which appeals to them. Anyhow, to the extent that he is right that there is a transfer of money from low income people to middle income people, the situation could be improved by certain changes in the financing. You don't have to do away with the entire social security system to rectify that.

But let me emphasize that the reason why the Office of Economic Opportunity and other such programs don't get appropriations, don't get support from the taxpayer, is simply that they do not appeal to the middle class, middle income person. True, if you are an economist, you may exclude all matters of politics from your thinking. But to do so is not reality, Milton. [Laughter.]

And so I say that the essence of social security, with its appeal to middle income people, is desirable and those things that are legitimately criticized about the system could easily be remedied by certain changes.

My major objection to the negative income tax as a complete substitute for social security is that I am convinced that, in the United States, a program that deals only with the poor will end up being a poor program. There is every evidence that this is true. Ever since the Elizabethan Poor Law of 1601, programs only for the poor have been lousy, no good, *poor* programs. And a program that is only for the poor—one that has nothing in it for the middle income and the upper income—is, in the long run, a program the American public won't support. This is why I think one must try to find a way to link the interests of all classes in these programs.

I would therefore argue that continuation of the social security system, reinforced through a guaranteed income, a negative income tax, or some other form of national welfare system, is more in keeping with American free enterprise and with our political system than dumping social security and substituting a poor program only for poor people—which, in the end, would not give security to poor people either. [Applause.]

MILTON FRIEDMAN

As many of you probably know, there are quite a number of state legislatures that at one time or another have passed a law saying that the value of Pi should be three. [Laughter.] According to Mr. Cohen's analysis of the meaning of insurance, that means that Pi is now three.

I fully recognize that insurance does not mean that individual payments are equal to individual benefits, but, rather, that individual payments have an actuarial equivalent in the benefits that are associated with them. I assure you that based on that definition of insurance, which is the definition that is widely accepted and used, there is very, very little connection between social security as it is now set up and any kind of an insurance program you can imagine.

Of course, combining the tax element and the benefit element into one system does serve a purpose. It serves a political purpose. It serves the political purpose of getting people to accept something under false pretenses. It serves the purpose of selling people a program they would not buy if they knew what they were buying. This is the political function of linking them together and this is what I meant when I said it was a triumph of imaginative packaging.

But as an economic matter, as a political matter (except as that means merely getting bills passed), the combining of the two halves is not, I am sorry to say, anything like the ineffable chemistry of combining man and woman. [Laughter.]

I am really a little puzzled by the argument Mr. Cohen makes here and in his paper that hinges around the phrase "a program for the poor will most likely be a poor program." His argument seems to be that he recognizes that the social security program provides disproportionate benefits to the middle class but that this is the price of getting it enacted. What puzzles me is this. Are we really helping poor people by saying to them "Here is a program under which we will take two dollars from you and give you one back, and we can get that program passed, but we can't get a program passed which will take a dollar from you and give you a dollar back"?

If that is the case, it seems to me that if I were one of those poor people—if I were one of the people to whom Mr. Cohen is saying "Don't worry, we'll take care of you, we promise that for every two dollars we take from you, you will get one back"—I would repeat Thoreau's wonderful comment: "If I knew for a certainty that a man was coming to my house with the conscious design of doing me good, I should run for my life." [Laughter.]

I think what is fundamentally at the bottom of the difference between Mr. Cohen and me—and here I agree with him—is not economic analysis. Rather it is basic philosophy.

There is a fundamental difference between the two philosophies, his and mine. One philosophy is that of a society in which the ultimate entity is the individual, a society resting upon the idea that people are responsible for themselves and for those close to them, that moral responsibility is an individual responsibility that has to be discharged personally and cannot be discharged by paying taxes levied by Congress. That is one view; that is my view.

Mr. Cohen's view, one which unfortunately is very widely held today, is different. It treats the nation not as a collection of individuals and of the groups which individuals separately value, but as an organic unit. In his paper, Mr. Cohen says: "I speak for the view that the nation should be generous toward the elderly." I would argue that the nation can't be generous to any-one. Only people can be generous. Generosity is a human, individual trait, not a collective trait. There is no generosity involved in my imposing taxes on *you* to help *him*. That is not generosity. [Laughter.]

But, nonetheless, underlying the social security view— and it is a view that is very widespread—is the idea that society is an organism, that an elite group within society knows what is good for other people better than they do for themselves, that this elite has a duty and a responsibility to induce people at large to pass the laws that will be good for them and that, in particular, it has the obligation to package this program in such an appealing way that they will adopt it, even if they would not adopt each of its parts separately.

Obviously, that is not the way Mr. Cohen would describe his philosophy. He is an eloquent man and describes it very well for himself. But it does seem to me that, at bottom, you do have these different views and that he is right in saying there is a far more fundamental issue at stake than the technical problems involved in the details of the program.

That fundamental issue is: As we look toward the future, do we want our society to develop in such a way that individuals separately will have greater responsibility, or do we want it to develop in such a way that the collective entity is more dominant and more omnipresent? Speaking for myself, I would say that our growing wealth, our growing income, makes it all the more possible for us to let individuals separately run their own lives. I would like to see us develop in a way which gives greater freedom to each one of us separately and which reduces the role of collective entities.

Thank you. [Applause.]

DISCUSSION

PETER LISAGOR, *Chicago Daily News* and moderator of the debate: The issue would seem to have been joined. Dean Cohen believes social security is sound, that its shortcomings can be cured by relatively small changes in the present system. Professor Friedman, to use his own words, wants to reform welfare and unwind social security.

We now turn to our panel of experts for their questions.

DOROTHY McCAMMAN, consultant, Senate Committee on Aging: I have a question for Mr. Friedman. With deferred costs last estimated by Bob Myers at $300 billion, what happens to the economy if the nation's workers are faced with the collapse of a system they believe in? How do they get their $300 billion out? What happens in the future to people's incentive to save through private pensions or through individual savings if whatever income they manage to put by makes them ineligible for income support because of a needs test?

MR. FRIEDMAN: You have asked a number of questions together. Let me take them one at a time.

First, with respect to the $300 billion—the figure probably is $500 billion or something like that now—

we already have that obligation. The only point is that it is not funded, it is not on paper. No economic fact would be changed by funding it. It must be paid somehow or other in the future, and what I'm proposing here is that we recognize in writing that we have the obligation, that we fund it in the form of an explicit government debt instead of an implicit one. In my paper, I have spelled out an arrangement for funding it so that workers would get the same benefits at the same time as they would under the existing rules.

What I want is to enable us to rule out further regressive taxation of the worker. There will be no collapse of the system—that's just another figment of the imagination. The fact is that you now have a social security debt. You now have that obligation. If funding it is going to collapse the system, the system should collapse now.

Second, the question of incentive to work and save. The facts are almost the reverse of what you suggest. Our present social security tax is a large disincentive. Over 10 percent of any worker's wage cost, at the low levels, which means up to $7,800 now and it will be higher later on—over 10 percent of his wage cost to his employer is taken out and sent to social security; the worker gets less than 90 percent of it.

Therefore, he does not have sufficient incentive now. Indeed, one of the great problems of providing sufficient incentive for a person to get off welfare is that, if he takes a job, then besides any reduction in his welfare benefits, he has to start paying social security taxes. He has to pay 10.8 percent of his wage cost in taxes and that raises the marginal rate.

I was astounded when I went through these figures. I had always thought that disincentive to work was associated with the high rates of the personal income tax. I am now persuaded that the social security tax is a greater disincentive to work than the personal income tax, because it hits people lower down; it hits people who have the alternative of relief and it hits them hard.

The social security tax is, for most people, decidedly higher than the personal income tax. That is why I think eliminating the payroll tax would add to people's incentives to work. This in turn would raise our total output, making it more feasible for people to put their own funds aside to provide for later benefits, for their own private pensions.

MR. COHEN: Might I comment on that? First, I don't think there's really any empirical evidence that Friedman can offer to show that the payroll tax has been a disincentive to individuals to work.

Secondly, if social security were abolished and the responsibility left to private enterprise, then the unions undoubtedly would have the same cost put on the employer and economy through collective bargaining, so the net economic effect would be exactly the same. If the unions didn't impose such a levy by negotiation, benefits would have to be paid out of general revenues in which case possibly the only way you'd get the money would be by raising the marginal income tax rate in the top bracket.

Now what I'd like to know from Professor Friedman is which of those two he recommends: unions bargaining with employers to finance benefits through privately imposed payroll levies or raising the marginal rate on the federal income tax back to 90 percent?

MR. FRIEDMAN: Neither. [Laughter.]

MR. COHEN: How are you going to get the money then?

MR. FRIEDMAN: The money for what, for paying the debt we have now accumulated?

MR. COHEN: No, no. For providing social security through the private enterprise system.

MR. FRIEDMAN: In the first place, there is an enormous difference between social security on the one hand and individuals separately paying over part of their wages to buy a pension which they separately desire on the other. The latter is not a disincentive. If I spend some of my income to buy a pension of my own free will, that's part of my payment, not a disincentive. The disincentive arises under social security because the payroll tax, which is deducted from my salary, has a very minor relation to any benefit I will subsequently get.

MR. COHEN: But you're living in an unreal world, Professor Friedman. You know that if social security were repealed, the matter of providing pensions wouldn't be left to each individual John Jones. The unions would try to handle it through bargaining with employers, and they would put the cost entirely on the employer, which would have exactly the same economic effect as it has now under present arrangements. And you'd have larger reserves than you have now. So what would you have gained economically? You'd have the same disincentive.

MR. FRIEDMAN: What you are saying is wrong.

It is wrong first, because fewer than 25 percent of workers are unionized today; most workers are not.

It is wrong, second, because the unions would bargain only for such pension benefits as the workers—their union members—would prefer. The union leaders are, after all, responsible to the employees—they are the agents of their own members. They would bargain for only such benefits as their own members wanted to have in the form of pensions rather than in the form of cash.

In the third place, of course, both under social security and under union arrangements, there is no important difference to the employee whether, in the first instance, the sum is paid by the employer or by the employee.

MR. COHEN: I agree. Therefore, the unions and others would put the whole cost on the employer.

MR. FRIEDMAN: You agree? No, no, I have to stop you because this is an historic moment. [Laughter.] Mr. Cohen—in every single thing I've ever seen that he has written on this subject—has denied the proposition he just agreed to. He agreed now—

MR. COHEN: I have never denied it. You have never seen or heard me deny it. And I don't justify it on economic grounds; I defend it on the basis of aesthetic logic, which you don't recognize. [Laughter.]

MR. FRIEDMAN: Excuse me, I have seen things written under your name in which you related the benefits received by the individual to the employee tax without mentioning the employer tax. The implication was that that employer tax did not count in relating individual payments to individual benefits.

MR. COHEN: No, sir. What you have seen but not correctly interpreted is the fact that the employee contribution is used as a measure of equity in the system. But there is also such a thing as social adequacy.

If you read the famous 1937 essay written by Reinhard Hohaus, vice president of Metropolitan Life Insurance Company, on equity and social adequacy in social insurance, you'll see that both elements are given some weight. I completely support the idea that in social insurance you have two elements: an equity concept and a social concept. Balancing them is the art that has made social security an acceptable system.

MR. FRIEDMAN: We are talking at cross-purposes. I want to ask you a simpler question, a very simple question. Do you agree that the division of the total tax between a tax on the employer and a tax on the employee has little or no effect on who actually pays it?

MR. COHEN: That is correct; so what?

MR. FRIEDMAN: Okay, if that is correct—

MR. COHEN: So what do you draw from that?

MR. FRIEDMAN: As I say, I regard this as an historic moment because I have never seen that admission in any social security document or in any document written by you. That admission means that many of the statements made by you and by the Social Security Administration about the relation of benefits to amounts paid are, to put it plainly, pure hogwash.

MR. COHEN: You know, there's an old Yiddish term called chutzpah. [Laughter.]

MR. FRIEDMAN: And you and I both have our share.

MR. COHEN: Professor Friedman demonstrates chutzpah better than anyone else I know. When he disagrees with anything somebody has said, he says, "You're not meeting my definition." The point is simply that the social security system meets the test of insurance, it meets the test of equity, and it meets the test of social adequacy. And as to the fact that he doesn't agree with it—well, he's not Congress, he's not the American people. He's only an economist. [Laughter.]

MR. FRIEDMAN: Thank God for small favors. [Laughter.]

THEODOR SCHUCHAT, North American Newspaper Alliance: Professor Friedman, in your paper and in your remarks you have stated that public assistance was intended as a temporary program for persons in distress, to be largely phased out as employment improved and as social security matured. Then you say there is no sign that social security has displaced assistance, that both are at all-time highs, et cetera.

Now aren't you mixing apples with oranges here? Isn't it a fact that the portion of the public assistance program that deals with the same hazards as the social security program—that is, old age, the orphan, premature death of family breadwinners, and so on—isn't it a fact that the portions of the public assistance rolls reflecting these problems have declined markedly? To that extent, hasn't the social security system accomplished what it set out to do?

The social security system was not created, nor has it ever tried, to take care of family breakup due to divorce and desertion. Those are the factors which have made the public assistance rolls leap to an all-time high.

MR. FRIEDMAN: There is no doubt that some of the people who are receiving benefits under social security are people who, in the absence of social security, might be on the public assistance rolls. That's quite right. And I wouldn't want to argue for a moment that there isn't some interchange or competition between the two.

Let me quote a phrase in Mr. Cohen's paper which says essentially the same thing as I have been saying about the original intent of social security. In his section III, he states: "The 1935 decision was to accept plan (2) . . . [with] the hope . . . that the welfare portion for the aged would ultimately wither away."

Now the initial idea was that old age and unemployment, the identifiable risks, were the major source of need for public assistance and that, if those were adequately taken care of, the need for public assistance would largely wither away and disappear.

All I am trying to say here is that it hasn't happened that way; on the contrary, public assistance has grown. It might be that it would have grown still more rapidly if there had been no social security system, but that is by no means clear.

The reason it's not clear is that, while there are some people now receiving benefits under social security who would otherwise be on public assistance, there may well be some people receiving public assistance who would not be if there had been no social security program extracting taxes from them. You must look at that side of it as well as the benefits they received.

Up to now, the persons who have retired have received much more from social security than they ever individually paid into it in taxes. That's the difference between the young and the old. So, undoubtedly, today social security keeps more people off the public assistance rolls than it adds to them, but it's not necessarily true that that's going to continue to be the case.

VINCENT BURKE, *Los Angeles Times:* We had a little argument down here relating to the topic of this debate, "Social Security—Universal or Selective?" As I understand it, Mr. Friedman is saying social security should be universal and Mr. Cohen is saying it should be selective. Did I get it straight?

MR. FRIEDMAN: No, it's the other way around. I'm saying welfare should be universal but that social security should be selective, that is, that you should select out and make payments to only those who demonstrate a need through an income test.

MR. BURKE: But using social security in the broad sense of a program to help poor people—in that sense, is Mr. Friedman saying, Yes, and are you, Mr. Cohen, saying, No? [Laughter.]

MR. COHEN: I am saying that social security, in the course of time, for the risks of old age, survivors and disability, should be universal in the sense that it should cover the total population and provide the basic floor of protection for those three risks.

MR. BURKE: It should remain non-universal, in other words?

MR. COHEN: No, it should be universal.

MR. BURKE: You know, we have a lot of poor people who aren't covered.

MR. COHEN: But, in the course of time, they will be covered.

MR. FRIEDMAN: How do you cover them, if they don't ever pay a social security tax?

MR. COHEN: There are, it is true, a few people who are not covered by social security, but over 92 percent are, and, in the course of a lifetime, most of the rest, if not all of them, will be also covered.

MR. BURKE: How do you cover an AFDC mother who is not working?

MR. COHEN: Oh, we agreed that we're only talking about the risks of old age, survivors and disability. There is no possibility of having an insurance system to cover illegitimacy that I know of.

VOICES: Why not?

MR. COHEN: Because of what insurance experts call the moral hazard. Because you cannot set up an insurance program where a man can secure benefits for his wife by leaving the home. No insurance company—no private insurance company will insure against that, nor will a social security system. That's the reason. . . .

MR. FRIEDMAN: To get back to the title of this debate, I have been interpreting it more nearly your way. That's why I linked social security with public assistance, looking not particularly to the problem of people who are poor because of age but simply to people who are poor. That's why I have combined the two, and I agree with your interpretation. In your sense of the term, I'd be for universalizing social security but as an assistance program rather than as insurance, because it isn't an insurance program. It really is a misnomer to speak of social security as insurance in any sense in which that word is equally applicable to life insurance, to fire insurance—

MR. COHEN: He's absolutely wrong but he persists in his error. [Laughter.]

MR. FRIEDMAN: Do you want to know what chutzpah really is? [Laughter.]

MR. COHEN: Yes, sir, it's a Professor Friedman telling the United States what to do.

MR. FRIEDMAN: Chutzpah describes the boy who is before the court for killing both his parents and who throws himself on the mercy of the court because he's an orphan. [Laughter.]

ROBERT MYERS, Temple University and formerly chief actuary, Social Security Administration: I have a few comments, and I'll try to keep them brief.

First of all, I'm in the happy or unhappy position of both agreeing and disagreeing with both debaters.

As for Mr. Cohen, I agree completely with him as to the desirability of the social insurance approach, but I disagree completely as to the benefit level. In essence, I think he's saying that since the minimum benefit should be about double what it is now, the entire benefit structure should be raised accordingly—because you have to maintain some spread between the lowest benefits and the highest. In my view, if the benefit level were doubled, it would mean the virtual end of all the private sector economic security activities to which Mr. Cohen pays lip service.

I also disagree with Mr. Cohen's proposal that supplementary public assistance should ultimately account for only one percent of total social security payments. I think a more realistic limit would be 10 percent—and, if I may say so, I think Mr. Cohen made a mistake when he said the original intent of the Social Security Act was

that public assistance should wither away; rather it was
that it should recede to a relatively low level.

Now, as for Dr. Friedman, I agree heartily with
him that the individual-insurance or individual-equity
aspects of social insurance have been overplayed, but I
would insist that social insurance or social security has
insurance aspects to it—it's different from private insurance, and necessarily so. I also agree completely with
Dr. Friedman on the importance of individual and family responsibility—and such responsibility would certainly suffer if all social security-type activities were
taken over by the government.

I disagree with him, however, about the inequity to
younger workers. I think, although it's true that the
employer taxes in the aggregate are paid by the employees or by the population, they are not really assignable individually, any more than is the case with any
other employee benefits. In group life insurance or
group pensions, the employer pays much more for the
older employee than for the younger employee. In a
maternity benefit plan, the younger worker gets far
more protection and value than the older worker does
from the employer. The employer taxes just are not
individually assignable.

Now—and this is even more important—I don't agree
with the public assistance emphasis in Dr. Friedman's
approach. I think there should be a floor of protection
provided through social insurance. I think people should
build on it through their own efforts and those of their

employers. But I'm afraid the public assistance approach will destroy incentives for private sector activities in the economic security field.

And, finally, I have some serious hesitations about Dr. Friedman's proposed methods for dismantling social security. I see great difficulties, if not impossibilities, in determining the earned benefits and deciding what the guiding concepts are. Also, there would be problems about funding, because of the huge amounts involved. Furthermore, I can't quite understand, and therefore I'd like to see a real quantitative demonstration of, Dr. Friedman's thesis that social security transfers money from the poor to the middle class. I think it does just the opposite because of the heavily weighted benefit formula.

MR. FRIEDMAN: I agree with the implication of Mr. Myers' final comment that it's extremely difficult to get a really satisfactory analysis of the redistribution involved in social security.

If it weren't for the fact that there is some variation of benefits in relation to average earnings, it would be very clear. I take it you would agree completely with the point I've made in my paper—that low income people start working earlier and thus pay into the system longer, have a shorter life expectancy and thus are less likely to receive benefits for as long a time, that the tax is regressive on lower incomes.

The only counterweight to this is the extent to which benefits are related to earnings, and it's not possible to say with absolute certainty what the effect of this is. Maybe I am wrong, but the more I have looked at it—and I haven't looked at it as much as you have so your judgment is probably better than mine—the more it has seemed to me that this earnings-related aspect of the total situation is too small to offset the other factors in the picture which tend to redistribute income from lower income people to higher income people.

I should have mentioned something else. The fact that benefits paid are not subject to income tax is extremely important for the upper income classes. The fact that the so-called employer contribution is not subject to the individual income tax is another factor.

Maybe I'm wrong, and I would like to see a really satisfactory analysis of it, but my judgment has been that on the whole these elements more than offset the earnings-related benefit.

Now let me go back to just one other comment that Mr. Myers made. I really don't understand his comment about the employer tax at all. It may be that the benefits are not individually attributable but the tax paid by the employer on behalf of each employee is individually attributable. If I am receiving a wage of $100 a week and the employer is paying—let's say it's 5 percent—a 5 percent tax, then he is paying $5 on my account and my wage cost to him is $105. What the employer is paying is clear. What the employee is getting may not be. In the case of the social security tax, isn't that correct? Isn't what the employer is paying perfectly attributable to the individual? If an employer hires me, he has to pay $105. He has to add $105 to his costs rather than $100. That's his wage cost. Now in what sense is that not individually attributable?

MR. MYERS: I would say it's not individually attributable just like the situation when an actuary tells an employer with a private pension plan, "This pension plan is going to cost you 6 percent of your payroll" and so the employer puts up 6 percent of each employee's salary. But that doesn't mean that each employee gets the value of that 6 percent. Rather, it's pooled.

MR. FRIEDMAN: You're talking about what the employee gets, but I'm talking about what it costs the employer to hire an employee. From that point of view, it couldn't make the slightest bit of difference to the employer whether he pays me $105 in cash and I pay $10 over to social security as a tax imposed on me or he pays me $95 and sends a $10 check to social security. That distinction is meaningless.

Therefore, the tax the employer pays is individually attributable in the same way as the employee tax. I can't see the difference.

MR. COHEN: I think Mr. Friedman is correct and Mr. Myers, too, in this case.

JOHN HERLING, National Newspaper Syndicate: Another history-making moment. [Laughter.]

MR. COHEN: Yes. Mr. Friedman is talking about it from the standpoint of costs to the employer and he is correct. Mr. Myers is talking about it in connection with the so-called actuarial determination of the relationship of the contribution to the benefit. Mr. Myers is speaking as an actuary in that he looks at the costs for the entire group of people as a single expense, the way group insurance does, without relating either costs or benefits to the individual specifically. So I think both are correct.

Now let me add a comment in connection with Mr. Myers' views on social security payment levels. He has stated a number of times that he thinks the payment levels I recommend are too high and would drive the private sector out of existence.

First, the record of the past 35 years shows that there is no basis in the past for thinking so. His point of view is purely speculative about the future. As a matter of fact, if anything, social security has encouraged private pension plans, private savings, private initiative, private plans of all sorts. Home ownership is higher now, savings are higher, and there are more private pension plans than ever before. Looking at it historically, there is very little basis for Mr. Myers' conclusion.

Second, as far as the future is concerned, my recommendations for the increase in benefits are based upon the hypothesis that the gross national product will continue to increase in the future approximately as it has since 1935, which is to say a little over 4 percent compounded annually. I see no reason not to have faith that our present free enterprise system is going to con-

tinue and I believe we have a responsibility to see to it
that the people who are old, the people who are sick, the
people who retire, the survivors and the disabled share
in the increased productivity of the nation.

Social security is a political and accounting system
whereby people who have participated in the life of our
society share, during their nonproductive years, with
those who are productive. Therefore, I believe the benefits will go up. They should go up. They will not rep-
resent a substantially increased burden on the economy
and they will not have an adverse effect on private pension plans.

JOHN PHILIP CARLSON, Committee on Government Operations of the House of Representatives: Mr.
Cohen, you placed considerable emphasis on public acceptance of the social security system. Do you see this
continuing after the first enthusiastic recipients—those
who, I think, probably get a better bargain out of social
security than future recipients will get—no longer dom-
inate the beneficiary group? Do you see this same public
acceptance continuing?

MR. COHEN: I believe that, as the payroll taxes go
up, there will be more resistance to future increases;
therefore, I believe that we will have to consider alternatives. I have written about several in my public
papers and some of them may be as follows:

—Increasing the payroll tax on the employers substantially above the present limit.

—Providing for a government subsidy.

—Perhaps reducing or rebating the tax on low income people.

—Perhaps having some type of guaranteed minimum payment akin to a negative income tax and building a doubledecker system in which you give X amount to everybody out of general revenue, somewhat as Mr. Friedman suggests, plus a variable benefit related to the individual's contribution.

There are a number of such possibilities, and in my opinion each of them might be introduced without losing the present general purpose and direction of the social security system.

MR. FRIEDMAN: I just want to ask one question of Mr. Cohen in this connection. He has been emphasizing the extent to which you can project the past into the future. Does he expect that the tax per person will continue to go up twice as fast as the benefits per person, as it has in the past 20 years? Because I think that's highly relevant to the question that was just asked.

The tax paid by covered persons has risen 7½ fold from 1950 to 1970 and the benefits paid have risen something like three fold. Do you think that that discrepancy will continue?

MR. COHEN: I don't know. Of course, during the same time marginal tax rates for people in higher income groups have been reduced from 90 percent. Under your proposal for more general revenues, you are pushing for higher marginal rates on higher income people. That's what your proposals are leading to.

MR. FRIEDMAN: I'm sorry—

MR. COHEN: That's not what you favor but that's what you're going to get.

MR. FRIEDMAN: It's not what I favor and it's not, I hope, what I shall get. And what you just said about the income tax is not correct because you are looking at nominal rates and not at real rates. Inflation has raised the burden of the income tax so that despite decreases in rates, the average effective rate paid under the personal income tax is higher today than at any time in our history, including the peak date in World War II.

GEORGE WATTLES, Postal Service Commission: Mr. Cohen, how do you ascertain whether private initiative and private pension funds are greater because of, or in spite of, social security? You have said private pension funds are growing. How do you know they wouldn't have grown twice as fast if you hadn't had social security?

MR. COHEN: They would have. They would have had to grow twice as fast if there weren't social security, because the social need would have been there. I do not deny that.

MR. WATTLES: Then social security has been a deterrent to the growth of private funds?

MR. COHEN: Certainly it's been a deterrent. Thank God, because, if you had nearly everyone in the United States covered only under a private pension plan, with huge reserves, or with little or no vesting, with the sort of things going on in some private plans, with the danger of a Studebaker company going bankrupt and leaving people without pension rights, you'd have a disaster in the United States. So I believe that the blend of social security, which is a minimum guarantee, with selective private pensions for companies and unions that can afford them is the best of both possible worlds.

PHILIP SHACKLETTE, St. Anselm's College: There are many people in my area who are going on retirement who are concerned about the fact that there is only $30 to $35 billion in the social security trust fund. Dr. Friedman mentioned that there is no guarantee that benefits will continue to be paid, because it will be up to future generations to take up the tab.

I was wondering whether, in order to provide additional funds, it would be wise to substitute a value-added tax which would possibly increase the trust fund from $35 billion up to a higher level and thus give stronger guarantees to the people of the country who are on social security and who may or may not get paid?

MR. COHEN: I don't think you need to do that. Let me say I agree with Professor Friedman and Mr. Myers that, if social security were a private insurance company, it would have to have reserves of $300 or $400 billion. But that's the whole point; it is not a private insurance company.

A private insurance company must assume that it

could go out of business at any time. Social security doesn't need to make that assumption. Social security is backed by the political, economic, constitutional system of our economy and our government. Therefore, you don't have to have a $300 or $400 or $500 billion reserve, and so, it's not necessary to introduce a value-added tax or any other tax to fund an additional reserve. I agree with the recent advisory council headed by former Secretary of HEW Arthur Fleming, a Republican in the Eisenhower administration, which reported that reserve equal to about one year's benefit is sufficient as a contingency fund.

The other guarantee, which I know Professor Friedman doesn't like, is the expectation of future contributions, or taxes as he prefers to call them, from the individuals covered by the system. That is the guarantee of social security.

MR. FRIEDMAN: As I prefer to call them! Do you really think that it is a straight, nonrhetorical description to call compulsory taxes "contributions"?

MR. COHEN: Congress has done so. Why should I say Congress is a liar? [Laughter.]

MR. FRIEDMAN: I rest my case. [Laughter.]

RICHARD WILBUR, minority counsel, House Committee on Ways and Means: I've been interested in the debate on the incidence of the employer's tax here tonight and I have to say, having listened to it through the years before the committee, that I think that tax actually does fall in large measure on the employee. Beyond the logic of it, too, there is the practical consideration that that's certainly the way the program is sold to the average person. You can see it in the literature Professor Friedman cited.

If you ask the average worker whether the tax his employer pays is on his behalf and should be taken into account in determining his individual equity, I don't think you'll find one worker in a hundred that won't answer yes. Therefore I think it's incumbent on public officials, when looking at the individual equity part of the system, to compute benefits not on the basis of the individual's own contributions but in terms of the way the program has been sold to him.

Now a question for Mr. Cohen. In reading his paper, I thought he was talking about a $150 minimum benefit either now or in the very near future, and not at some future date after the gross national product has increased 4 percent a year for, say, 30 years. In the latter case, of course, personal income would have increased, maybe even doubled and then the higher benefits would not be out of line with wages.

But I thought you were talking about now. If you were, if you doubled benefits now, it seems to me you'd have to double the taxes and they would have to go up to around 25 percent. If payroll taxes reached 25 percent, I think you would have a real problem of disincentives to work and then the old cycle of problems starts all over again. The system would not have matured and you would have destroyed quite a bit, if not all, of the relationship of ultimate benefits to current contributions. Maybe 30 years from now we'll know how to deal with that situation but isn't it true, as Dr. Friedman points out in his paper, that what we have is more like a chain letter than an insurance system?

What has to happen before we can say that the system has matured and the people who are contributing will get a benefit equitably reflecting their contributions and the employer's contributions?

MR. COHEN: In the first place, let me say this: as I recall our discussions with Representative Byrnes, ranking Republican on the Ways and Means Committee— and I believe Mr. Myers will recall this too—back in 1960 or '65, as the case may be, Mr. Byrnes accepted the point that the employer contribution is pooled and should not be attributable to individual employees. At his request, the law was modified to ensure that a man and wife at the maximum taxable earnings line would receive at least 50 percent of his earnings. As I recall it, I believe he considered that satisfactory to meet the equity concept.

I think Mr. Byrnes, on behalf of the Republicans, did recognize that, in this system, social adequacy and equity may be two contradictory principles. Still, I think, he felt the equity concept was realized. That doesn't deny the validity of Professor Friedman's point that the individual employer's social security obligation is a business expense. Both are true.

Let me say, secondly, that I believe this is an intelligent compromise or resolution of the two conflicting interests.

MR. WILBUR: Illogical though.

MR. COHEN: Well, lots of things in life are illogical but what's illogical to you is a matter of symmetry and artistry to somebody else. [Laughter.]

MR. WILBUR: That sounds like that Yiddish term to me.

MR. COHEN: Right. And in order to operate this economic system, we have to have lots of chutzpah, because, if we didn't have chutzpah you couldn't operate a free enterprise system.

Now, about the question of the $150 minimum benefit, I would recommend that you read the actuarial data in the report that was just put out by the Fleming Commission. It indicates, in my opinion, that one can substantially raise social security benefits over a period of time without raising payroll taxes as much as has been originally anticipated. Because, if you go on an assumption of constantly increasing wages rather than static wages, then I believe you can do more than we have done up to now.

And, secondly, my view about the timing of the $150 is, well, maybe two years, or maybe three or even five years, from now. When the Ways and Means Committee comes out with its report in connection with the welfare bill and, if it selects $150 a month three years from now as the basis for federalizing the adult categories in the welfare system, I'd be perfectly prepared to put the $150 for social security in effect just before the welfare payment becomes operative.

MR. WILBUR: Might I just make one more brief comment?

Without agreeing with everything you said on the second point, I just want to make one more comment on the first point and that is that I'm speaking for myself and not for Mr. Byrnes.

MR. COHEN: Oh, I understand that. I just wanted to indicate that I was on his side once in a while.

MR. WILBUR: I don't necessarily agree with your interpretation of what transpired in the committee meetings. But, without getting into that, it does seem to me that we, as people working for the government, are still stuck with the fundamental problem that, as you agree, we've sold the system on the basis that the employer's contribution is on the employee's behalf. That's also the logic of the situation.

So it seems to me a contradiction to turn around and argue that, by saying you get back 50 percent of what you paid in, we can justify it both in logic and because that's the way the system was sold. I think that somebody, sometime, has got to deal with that fundamental problem.

MR. BURKE: Mr. Cohen has told us that a program just for the poor is a poor program and Mr. Friedman, I think, has said that we should have a universal poor program. I wanted to ask both gentlemen how they define this poor program. Since Mr. Friedman wants to have a universal poor program, my question to him is: What kind of a universal poor program? Do you agree that a poor program would be poor?

My question to Mr. Cohen is: Are you saying that you believe this society will never have a program for a mother and children, legitimate or illegitimate, that is anything but poor and we must reconcile ourselves to that?

MR. COHEN: I think you have touched probably the fundamental difference between my view and Mr. Friedman's, because in principle I am not opposed to the concept of a negative income tax as a method of providing a guaranteed income for certain classes of people under certain circumstances. It's just that I believe it has to be either a transitional or a minimal type of program. I think this point will be demonstrated when the Ways and Means Committee reports out the welfare bill. These are the reasons: First, the bill will probably have a test of income and a test of resources, which, in the mind of the average person, is called a means test. Since the Elizabethan Poor Law of 1601, a means test has been anathema to most of the people in England and in the United States and all of this ragbag of programs, as Professor Friedman calls it, represents an effort to get away from the means test.

Secondly (and this too is likely to be demonstrated by the welfare reform bill), I don't think Congress will accept a plan for complete income distribution financed out of general revenues that doesn't include a work requirement test requiring mothers to go to work when they have young children, and/or other moral requirements—which again will be anathema to some people. This is one reason I'm skeptical about Professor Friedman's recommendation.

It's also why I believe payroll taxes—despite their regressivity, and despite all the other criticisms he makes —are valuable. They safeguard the statutory benefit as a matter of right. I don't justify this as a method of taxation. I only justify it as a moral and compassionate method of giving security to people so that they don't have to go through the humiliation of a means test, plus judgment by moral standards, plus resource tests—all of which they don't like.

MR. BURKE: Are you saying, though—do you agree that the AFDC mother who has no earnings record is consigned to a poor program, always, forever? Is that the way you analyze this thing?

MR. COHEN: I'm trying to be a realist. Are you asking me for my personal view, or for what the body politic thinks? I'm trying to be a realist.

MR. BURKE: I'm asking is this the way you analyze the society?

MR. COHEN: I analyze the society of 1971 that way. Now, as I said in my paper, maybe in 1981 or 1991—maybe in the year 2000, in a different society, under different circumstances, with a different gross national product—with the young people who are now coming up in control of the power structure, it might be different. But, at the present time, between 1971 and 1976, I do not see the possibility of having an adequate federal income guarantee for poor people out of general revenues with no restrictions of the sort I mentioned.

MR. FRIEDMAN: You notice that Mr. Cohen in listing those dates skipped a very important one. [Laughter.]

But let me go back and let me try to answer your question.

I believe that part of this is a play on words. What Mr. Cohen called a nonpoor program, I do not call a nonpoor program. I believe that the programs we have under social security are more properly described as poor programs. They are poor programs, from my point of view, because they are taking from some people and giving to others without the consent of those who are paying the bill.

But let me go more directly to your question and try, at the same time, to answer Mr. Cohen's statement. I believe that a program which is going to give income to people, which is going to give funds to people, should have a means test. I believe we have a responsibility to the taxpayer and not only to poor people.

I believe that the person who pays taxes has every right to require that, if he pays the taxes in order to help somebody, there be some evidence that that person needs help. And so I do not, myself, regard a means

test as in any way whatsoever an undesirable char-
acteristic of a program. But I do regard the means test
we have *now* as a very undesirable means test. A straight
income means test of the kind you would have under a
negative income tax is the right kind of a means test
and I think you should have it.

Now, with respect to whether you can get such
programs financed out of general revenue, I believe
that's a question of what we persuade people is right
or wrong. If we go around telling people that taxes
are contributions, stressing the fact that benefits have
risen threefold and not mentioning that taxes have
risen sevenfold, not emphasizing the lack of relationship between payments on the one hand and so-called
benefits on the other, then we shall persuade people
to do the wrong thing. Even the word benefits bothers
me. There are no benefits. There are subsidies. That
would be the correct, accurate term.

But if we tell people the facts and don't try to mislead them, then maybe we can get a decent program for
poor people. I believe we can, if the public at large is
properly informed.

Mr. Cohen says we can't get an income distribution
program out of general revenue without work requirements tests and/or other moral standards. Again, I
don't believe it's inappropriate to have a work feature
built-in as an incentive so that people will go to work
and will be able to keep a considerable fraction of their
income.

A program of that kind would be vastly less expensive than the ones we've now got. It would do a better job of helping people. In my view, the task of people like Mr. Cohen and myself is not to speculate about what people will do if they don't have leadership but to try to provide leadership in order to obtain the kind of good program that would achieve our objectives.

So I don't really agree that we have to have a poor program in a correct sense of the term poor. I believe that is a play on words.

MR. COHEN: I think Professor Friedman has misunderstood my point. I agree with him completely about the value of a work incentive feature in the sense of an income disregard that allows working welfare recipients to keep part of their wages. That was not what I meant. I was alluding to the amendments first introduced in 1967, and included in the legislation last year and this, which would require a mother to go to work and put her children in day care, even if she wants to stay home with them, or risk losing her income payments.

I agree about the incentive payment schedule—that if a mother goes to work, she should get more. But I do not agree that, in these programs paid out of general revenues, we ought to press every mother to decide between going to work and taking care of her children. I think that is an area of individual responsibility and I am shocked that the economists and other people you refer to have not risen to deal with that moral question, which I think is a very important one.

MR. FRIEDMAN: As you know, Mr. Cohen, I have never myself been in favor of that requirement. At the same time, if I face it honestly, I have to distinguish between what's a question of prudence and what's a question of morality. I believe that taxpayers have every right to set the conditions under which the money they pay out will be received. I believe that we do have to look at what we owe the taxpayers as well as what we owe the recipients. However, I think that the requirement is extremely unwise from a prudential point of view. I don't say it's morally wrong. But I think it's extremely unwise and undesirable to have the kind of work requirement that you spoke of.

SAR LEVITAN, George Washington University: Professor Friedman, you have been preaching the gospel of consumer sovereignty and I am fully in agreement with you but I'm wondering why social security is contrary to the gospel of capitalism and freedom. Why should it be consumer sovereignty if an individual, let's say, goes out and buys a monetary history of the United States or whatever he wants, but not be consumer sovereignty when a number of individuals band together and decide they want to have social security with some kind of future benefits paid by the government and for which they want to contribute? Or do you have some special knowledge that this is contrary to the will of the electorate of the United States?

MR. FRIEDMAN: I think you've asked not a simple

question but an extremely complicated question that goes to basic political philosophies. In the first place, I have not been saying in any way that we should violate the laws of the land or that the laws should be decided in another way. I've been trying to persuade the people that they ought to vote differently. That's trying to serve the same function with respect to consumer sovereignty as you define it as advertising serves with respect to consumer sovereignty in the private market.

But, much more fundamentally, I believe there is a philosophical difference between consumer sovereignty in which 100 percent of the people decide to join in a program and a situation in which 51 percent of the people impose taxes on the other 49 percent of the people. I don't believe the two really come under the same blueprint. And I think you do not believe so either. Taking your definition of consumer sovereignty, if 51 percent of the people vote to shoot the other 49 percent of the people, is that appropriate consumer sovereignty? You'd say, No, of course not.

MR. LEVITAN: I think that's not an appropriate similarity.

MR. FRIEDMAN: But exactly the same way, it is not an appropriate similarity to individual consumer sovereignty to say that consumer sovereignty has been exercised when 51 percent of the people vote to impose taxes on 100 percent of the people in order to pay benefits, let us say, to 100 percent of the people.

I favor majority rule as an expedient, because there are certain decisions that have to be made jointly and this is the least bad way of doing it. But I do not regard it as a principle; whereas, I do regard individual responsibility as a principle. The idea of using my resources to achieve my objectives, so long as I don't interfere with anybody else doing the same, I regard that as a value wholly different from the expedient of majority rule.

MR. COHEN: Individual responsibility may be defined as the principle which gives people freedom to starve, if they wish. I believe that there is a higher and nobler principle and that is the responsibility of the society for the well-being of its members.

As Mr. Friedman says, the commandments say "Honor thy father and mother," but they do not say honor thy father and thy mother as economists have predetermined. The commandment is to honor thy father and thy mother in all of the ways that you may think of, including the exercise of social responsibility —and that is what social security is. [Laughter.]

MODERATOR LISAGOR: I want to thank both of you for showing us what good debate means—and also what chutzpah means. And thanks, ladies and gentlemen, for your active participation. [Applause.]

APPENDIX AND NOTES
TO SECOND LECTURE

APPENDIX

Note 1

SUMMARY OF PRINCIPAL FEATURES OF OASDHI

1. The maximum annual wage base is $7,800. The 1971 bill increasing social security benefits raises this base to $9,000 effective January 1, 1972.

2. For OASI, the tax rate is 8.1 percent for employees and 6.075 percent for the self-employed. For OASDHI, the tax rate is 10.4 percent for employees and 7.5 percent for the self-employed.

3. For OASI, the maximum tax per year is $631.80 for employees and $473.85 for the self-employed. For OASDHI, it is $811.20 for employees and $585.00 for the self-employed.

4. The only important groups that are still not covered are federal government employees, railroad workers, and state and local government employees who have chosen not to join. The total number of persons not covered is approximately 5 million.

5. The minimum benefit was raised to $70.40 per month for a single person and to $105.60 for a retired

The data in this appendix was prepared and subsequently updated by Rosemary and Colin Campbell, Dartmouth College.

couple by the 1971 bill raising social security benefits. The maximum benefit was raised to approximately $210 per month for a single person and $315 for a retired couple.

6. Benefits (slightly reduced) may start at age 62 for retired workers and at age 60 for a survivor.

7. A retired wife is entitled to ½ her husband's benefit. A widow gets 82½ percent of her late husband's benefit.

8. A wife cannot receive *both* the benefit based on her earnings and her benefit as a wife.

9. After 65, a worker may earn up to $140 per month or $1,680 per year without loss of benefits. Benefits are reduced $1 for each $2 of earnings from $1,681 to $2,880 and $1 for each $1 of earnings in excess of $2,880 up to age 72.

10. The minimum period of covered work to qualify for benefits is 20 quarters for men retiring in 1971 and 17 quarters for women. Only $50 per quarter must be earned in order to qualify. For persons retiring in the future, up to 10 years' coverage will be required. For persons over 72 years of age, a period of covered employment is not required. They receive $48.30 per month if single or $72.45 for a retired couple under the 1971 bill.

11. Benefits are based on the "average monthly wage." This is the average of monthly wages on which social security taxes have been paid since 1951, excluding five years of lowest wages, but including months with zero wages in excess of the five years allowed. The March

1971 formula for computing benefits is:
90.01% of the first $110 of the average
monthly wage, plus 32.74% of the next $290,
plus 30.59% of the next $150, plus 35.96%
of the next $100.

12. There are benefits for dependent children and
parents of retired workers, widowers of covered women
workers, and divorced wives. Citizens of other countries
who no longer reside in the United States may receive
social security benefits, provided that their country
treats U.S. citizens in a like manner.

Note 2

TREATMENT OF FOREIGNERS BY OASDI [1]

1. Benefits are paid to foreigners living abroad who
have paid enough social security taxes to qualify. There
are some restrictions, but they do not amount to much.[2]

---

[1] Based on William F. Yoffee, "Benefits Paid Abroad Under OASDI," *Social
Security Bulletin*, XXXII (February 1969), pp. 29-39.

[2] U.S. citizens may receive OASDI benefits while residing abroad, unless they
are in a country to which the Treasury prohibits mailing the check because of
security considerations. Medicare payments do not cover medical services received
outside the U.S.

Full OASDI benefits are paid to non-citizens of the U.S. living abroad, if they
have sufficient coverage and if they are citizens of a country that (1) has a
treaty provision with the U.S. about these payments, or (2) has a social security
system that allows unrestricted payments to U.S. citizens outside the country.
If their country's system does not allow this, they are eligible for benefits for
only six consecutive months after leaving the U.S. until a calendar month is
again spent in the U.S.

Citizens of countries having no applicable pension system can receive full
benefits if they have 40 quarters of coverage or have resided in the U.S. for 10
years. If they have less coverage than this, the six-month rule applies to them.

2. The policy regarding foreigners is based on the myth that OASDI is an insurance system—that foreigners who worked in this country earned their benefits.

3. Although the number and amount of benefits paid abroad equals approximately 1 percent of the total, OASDI has left itself wide open to exploitation by foreigners to earn the favorably weighted minimum benefit of $70.40 per month if single or $105.60 if married.[3] Foreigners are currently eligible with only 20 quarters of covered employment and have to earn only $50 per quarter. Eventually, 40 quarters of coverage will be necessary.

4. Statistics on beneficiaries living abroad lump foreigners with U.S. citizens.[4] Between 1960 and 1967, the number of such beneficiaries almost doubled (from 100,500 to 196,300), whereas the number of OASDI beneficiaries in the entire system increased about 50 percent. As the following table shows, between 1953 and 1968, Mexico recorded the largest increase in OASDI beneficiaries of the 15 countries which comprise 85-90 percent of program operations abroad.

---

[3] The average benefit paid abroad has been significantly smaller than the average benefit for the program as a whole since 1961. "The available evidence seems to indicate . . . that new beneficiaries abroad are qualifying for smaller benefits than beneficiaries in the U.S." (p. 34.)

[4] A 1964 study indicated that approximately 39 percent of OASDI beneficiaries living abroad were U.S. citizens. An additional 13 percent were alien dependents of U.S. citizens.

BENEFICIARIES IN CURRENT PAYMENT STATUS AND AMOUNTS OF BENEFITS [5]

Country	December 1956		February 1968	
	Number of beneficiaries	Benefits (in thousands)	Number of beneficiaries	Benefits (in thousands)
Treaty exception countries				
Federal Republic of Germany	2,388	$144.7	11,918	$1,097.0
Greece	5,558	305.6	15,218	1,228.0
Ireland	1,542	90.5	4,422	388.7
Italy	14,659	815.8	36,464	2,999.3
Japan	1,755	95.0	4,580	364.0
Social insurance or pension system exception countries (December 1967)				
Canada (from January 1966)	8,462	$412.3	28,064	$2,191.6
Philippines (from June 1960)	4,170	139.7	18,002	935.0
Spain (from May 1966)	1,243	77.6	5,430	479.2
United Kingdom	3,049	177.0	9,299	830.4
Yugoslavia	1,743	94.7	4,775	393.6
Countries meeting neither exception (December 1967)				
France	608	$ 35.7	2,488	$ 228.4
Mexico	1,723	93.0	15,232	846.0
Norway	1,411	82.7	4,493	408.2
Portugal	1,156	64.7	4,638	364.8
Sweden	1,619	101.8	4,372	412.0

[5] Yoffee, "Benefits Paid Abroad Under OASDI," Table 5.

Table 1-A

OASI AND OASDHI TAX COLLECTIONS AS A PERCENT OF TOTAL COVERED U.S. WAGES AND SALARIES, 1940-1969

Year	Total Covered Wages and Salaries [1] (in billions)	OASI Tax Collections (in millions)	OASI Taxes as % of Covered Wages and Salaries	OASDHI Tax Collections (in millions)	OASDHI Taxes as % of Covered Wages and Salaries
1940	$35.6	$ 325	0.9	—	—
1941	45.3	789	1.7	—	—
1942	58.0	1,012	1.7	—	—
1943	69.4	1,239	1.8	—	—
1944	73.1	1,316	1.8	—	—
1945	71.3	1,285	1.8	—	—
1946	79.0	1,295	1.6	—	—
1947	92.1	1,557	1.7	—	—
1948	101.9	1,685	1.7	—	—
1949	99.6	1,666	1.7	—	—
1950	109.4	2,667	2.4	—	—
1951	147.5	3,363	2.3	—	—
1952	158.1	3,819	2.4	—	—
1953	170.9	3,945	2.3	—	—
1954	169.9	5,163	3.0	—	—
1955	193.8	5,713	2.9	—	—
1956	214.3	6,172	2.9	—	—
1957	231.3	6,825	3.0	$7,527	3.3
1958	233.9	7,566	3.2	8,532	3.6
1959	252.2	8,052	3.2	8,943	3.5
1960	263.4	10,866	4.1	11,876	4.5
1961	268.7	11,285	4.2	12,323	4.6
1962	287.2	12,059	4.2	13,105	4.6
1963	299.8	14.541	4.9	15,640	5.2
1964	321.9	15,689	4.9	16,843	5.2
1965	348.5	16,017	4.6	17,205	4.9
1966	387.8	20,580	5.3	24,444	6.3
1967	417.8	23,138	5.5	28,576	6.8
1968	456.3	23,719	5.2	31,151	6.8
1969	501.3	27,947	5.6	36,019	7.2

[1] Covered wages and salaries include earnings of self-employed (starting 1951), and wages and salaries of employees; they exclude wages of uncovered federal employees, railroad workers, and state and local government employees.

Source: Based on *Social Security Bulletin, Annual Statistical Supplement*, 1969, Tables 6, 28, 29, and 30.

Table 1-B
OASI AND OASDHI TAX COLLECTIONS AS A PERCENT
OF TOTAL U.S. WAGES AND SALARIES, 1937-1970

Year	Total Wages and Salaries (in billions)	OASI Tax Collections (in millions)	OASI Taxes as % of Wages and Salaries	OASDHI Tax Collections (in millions)	OASDHI Taxes as % of Wages and Salaries
1937	$46.1	$ 765	1.7	—	—
1938	43.0	360	0.8	—	—
1939	45.9	580	1.3	—	—
1940	49.8	325	0.7	—	—
1941	62.1	789	1.3	—	—
1942	82.1	1,012	1.2	—	—
1943	105.8	1,239	1.2	—	—
1944	116.7	1,316	1.1	—	—
1945	117.5	1,285	1.1	—	—
1946	112.0	1,295	1.2	—	—
1947	123.0	1,557	1.3	—	—
1948	135.4	1,685	1.2	—	—
1949	134.5	1,666	1.2	—	—
1950	146.8	2,667	1.8	—	—
1951	171.1	3,363	2.0	—	—
1952	185.1	3,819	2.1	—	—
1953	198.3	3,945	2.0	—	—
1954	196.5	5,163	2.6	—	—
1955	211.3	5,713	2.7	—	—
1956	227.8	6,172	2.7	—	—
1957	238.7	6,825	2.9	$7,527	3.2
1958	239.9	7,566	3.2	8,532	3.6
1959	258.2	8,052	3.1	8,943	3.5
1960	270.8	10,866	4.0	11,876	4.4
1961	278.1	11,285	4.1	12,323	4.4
1962	296.1	12,059	4.1	13,105	4.4
1963	311.1	14,541	4.7	15,640	5.0
1964	333.7	15,689	4.7	16,843	5.0
1965	358.9	16,017	4.5	17,205	4.8
1966	394.5	20,580	5.2	24,444	6.2
1967	423.1	23,138	5.5	28,576	6.8
1968	464.9	23,719	5.1	31,151	6.7
1969	509.6	27,947	5.5	36,019	7.1
1970	541.4	30,256	5.6	39,618	7.3

Source: *Economic Report of the President* (1972), Table B-12; and Table 1-A above.

Table 2-A
OASI AND OASDHI TAX COLLECTIONS AS A PERCENT
OF PERSONAL SAVING

Year	Total Personal Saving (in billions)	OASI Tax Collections (in millions)	OASI Taxes as % of Personal Saving	OASDHI Tax Collections (in millions)	OASDHI Taxes as % of Personal Saving
1937	$ 3.8	$ 765	20.1	—	—
1938	0.7	360	51.4	—	—
1939	2.6	580	22.3	—	—
1940	3.8	325	8.6	—	—
1941	11.0	789	7.2	—	—
1942	27.6	1,012	3.7	—	—
1943	33.4	1,239	3.7	—	—
1944	37.3	1,316	3.5	—	—
1945	29.6	1,285	4.3	—	—
1946	15.2	1,295	8.5	—	—
1947	7.3	1,557	21.3	—	—
1948	13.4	1,685	12.6	—	—
1949	9.4	1,666	17.7	—	—
1950	13.1	2,667	20.4	—	—
1951	17.3	3,363	19.4	—	—
1952	18.1	3,819	21.0	—	—
1953	18.3	3,945	21.6	—	—
1954	16.4	5,163	31.5	—	—
1955	15.8	5,713	36.2	—	—
1956	20.6	6,172	30.0	—	—
1957	20.7	6,825	33.0	$ 7,527	36.4
1958	22.3	7,566	33.9	8,532	38.3
1959	19.1	8,052	42.2	8,943	46.8
1960	17.0	10,866	63.9	11,876	69.9
1961	21.2	11,285	53.2	12,323	58.1
1962	21.6	12,059	55.8	13,105	60.7
1963	19.9	14,541	73.1	15,640	78.6
1964	26.2	15,689	59.9	16,843	64.3
1965	28.4	16,017	56.3	17,205	60.6
1966	32.5	20,580	63.3	24,444	75.2
1967	40.4	23,138	57.3	28,576	70.7
1968	39.8	23,719	59.6	31,151	78.3
1969	37.9	27,947	73.7	36,019	95.0
1970	54.1	30,256	55.9	39,618	73.2

Source: Based on *Economic Report of the President* (1972), Table B-18; *Social Security Bulletin, Annual Statistical Supplement,* 1969, pp. 45-47; and *Social Security Bulletin* (November 1970 and August 1971), Tables M-5, M-6 and M-7.

Table 2-B

OASI AND OASDHI TAX COLLECTIONS AS A PERCENT OF PERSONAL AND BUSINESS SAVING

Year	Total Personal and Business Saving [1] (in billions)	OASI Tax Collections (in millions)	OASI Taxes as % of Total Saving	OASDHI Tax Collections (in millions)	OASDHI Taxes as % of Total Saving
1937	—	$ 765	—	—	—
1938	—	360	—	—	—
1939	$ 3.7	580	15.7	—	—
1940	6.8	325	4.8	—	—
1941	14.2	789	5.6	—	—
1942	32.3	1,012	3.1	—	—
1943	39.2	1,239	3.2	—	—
1944	43.5	1,316	3.0	—	—
1945	33.4	1,285	3.8	—	—
1946	19.8	1,295	6.5	—	—
1947	15.3	1,557	10.2	—	—
1948	26.8	1,685	6.3	—	—
1949	22.6	1,666	7.4	—	—
1950	24.1	2,667	11.1	—	—
1951	29.1	3,363	11.6	—	—
1952	30.1	3,819	12.7	—	—
1953	28.8	3,945	13.7	—	—
1954	27.4	5,163	18.8	—	—
1955	30.6	5,713	18.7	—	—
1956	33.5	6,172	18.4	—	—
1957	33.4	6,825	20.4	$ 7,527	22.5
1958	32.8	7,566	23.1	8,532	26.0
1959	34.5	8,052	23.3	8,943	25.9
1960	30.4	10,866	35.7	11,876	39.1
1961	34.7	11,285	32.5	12,323	35.5
1962	37.9	12,059	31.8	13,105	34.6
1963	36.0	14,541	40.4	15,640	43.4
1964	46.3	15,689	33.9	16,843	36.4
1965	53.4	16,017	30.0	17,205	32.2
1966	59.8	20,580	34.4	24,444	40.9
1967	64.6	23,138	35.8	28,576	44.2
1968	60.7	23,719	39.1	3,1,151	51.3
1969	52.4	27,947	53.3	36,019	68.7
1970	65.8	30,256	46.0	39,618	60.2

[1] Business saving includes undistributed corporate profits plus inventory adjustment.

Source: Table 2-A. Also based on *Handbook of Basic Economic Statistics*, January 1972 (Washington, D.C., Economic Statistics Bureau), p. 234.

Table 3

NUMBER OF BENEFICIARIES OF OASDHI CASH PAYMENTS, 1940-1970
(in thousands)

December 31	OASDHI Beneficiaries [1]			
	Retirement [2]	Disability	Survivor	Total
1940	148	—	74	222
1941	266	—	167	433
1942	347	—	252	599
1943	406	—	342	748
1944	504	—	451	955
1945	691	—	597	1,288
1946	936	—	707	1,643
1947	1,166	—	812	1,978
1948	1,395	—	920	2,315
1949	1,709	—	1,034	2,743
1950	2,326	—	1,152	3,478
1951	2,993	—	1,386	4,379
1952	3,456	—	1,569	5,025
1953	4,200	—	1,781	5,981
1954	4,898	—	1,989	6,887
1955	5,788	—	2,172	7,960
1956	6,677	—	2,451	9,128
1957	8,205	150	2,774	11,129
1958	9,148	268	3,015	12,431
1959	9,932	460	3,312	13,704
1960	10,599	687	3,558	14,844
1961	11,655	1,027	3,812	16,494
1962	12,675	1,275	4,104	18,053
1963	13,262	1,452	4,321	19,035
1964	13,697	1,563	4,539	19,799
1965	14,175	1,739	4,953	20,867
1966	15,437	1,970	5,360	22,767
1967	15,907	2,141	5,659	23,707
1968	16,264	2,335	5,963	24,562
1969	16,595	2,488	6,229	25,312
1970	17,100	2,666	6,469	26,235

[1] Includes dependents for retirement and disability.
[2] Beginning October 1966, includes special benefits authorized by 1966 legislation for persons aged 72 and over and not insured under the regular or transitional provisions of the Social Security Act.
Source: *Social Security Bulletin* (April 1971), Table M-3, p. 42.

Table 4

MAXIMUM AND MINIMUM OASI BENEFITS, TO PRIMARY BENEFICIARY, 1939-1971

Date of Act	Maximum Benefit Eventually Receivable Under Formula [1]	Maximum Currently Receivable	Average Monthly Benefit	Minimum Benefit
1939	$ 45.60 [2]	$ 41.20 [3]	$ 22.60 [3]	$ 10.00 [3]
1950	80.00	68.50	43.86	20.00
1952	85.00	85.00	49.25	25.00
1954	108.50	108.50	59.14	30.00
1958	127.00	116.00	66.35	33.00
1961	127.00	116.00	75.65	40.00
1965	168.00	132.00	83.92	44.00
1967	218.00	157.00	85.37	55.00
1969	250.70	190.00	100.40	64.00
1971	295.40	213.10	126.00 [4]	70.40

[1] Under the 1939 act, benefits were to be increased 1 percent for each year worked in covered employment. Thus the maximum amount eventually receivable was larger than that currently receivable. Between 1951 and 1953, these two figures were the same. Since 1955 they have differed because of increases in the maximum wage base used to compute benefits.

[2] Effective maximum; not specified in act.

[3] Starting in 1940.

[4] Approximate.

Source: Based on *Social Security Bulletin* (January 1972), Table M-13; and *Social Security Bulletin, Annual Statistical Supplement*, 1961, p. 7, Table 9, and 1969, p. 15.

Table 5

AVERAGE OASDHI MONTHLY CASH BENEFITS, BY TYPE OF BENEFICIARY, 1940-1970

Period	Retired workers and their dependents			Survivors of deceased workers				Disabled workers and their dependents			Persons with special age-72 benefits[8]
	Retired workers[1]	Wives and husbands[1,2]	Children[3]	Children[3]	Widowed mothers[4]	Widows and widowers[1,5]	Parents[1]	Disabled workers[6]	Wives and husbands[7]	Children[3]	
Average benefits in current-payment status at end of period											
1940	$22.60	$12.13	$ 9.70	$12.56	$19.61	$20.28	$13.09	—	—	—	—
1945	24.19	12.82	11.74	12.48	19.83	20.19	13.06	—	—	—	—
1950	43.86	23.60	17.05	28.43	34.24	36.54	36.69	—	—	—	—
1955	61.90	33.07	20.01	38.12	45.91	48.69	49.93	—	—	—	—
1960	74.04	38.72	28.25	51.37	59.29	57.68	60.31	$89.31	$34.41	$30.21	—
1961	75.65	39.45	27.52	52.74	59.38	64.91	67.15	89.59	33.09	29.13	—
1962	76.19	39.62	27.39	53.57	59.38	65.88	68.18	89.99	32.41	28.56	—
1963	76.88	39.94	27.85	54.33	59.43	66.84	69.11	90.59	32.23	28.39	—
1964	77.57	40.23	28.13	54.99	59.40	67.85	70.05	91.12	32.23	28.48	—
1965	83.92	43.63	31.98	61.26	65.45	73.75	76.03	97.76	34.96	31.61	—
1966	84.35	43.81	32.72	61.84	65.57	74.10	76.48	98.09	34.51	31.34	$34.33
1967	85.37	44.24	33.10	62.57	65.86	74.99	77.23	98.43	34.28	31.38	34.19
1968	98.86	51.21	38.12	70.85	74.93	86.43	88.21	111.86	38.26	34.79	39.20
1969	100.40	51.88	38.63	71.10	75.09	87.27	88.95	112.73	38.13	34.64	39.20
1970	118.10	61.19	44.85	82.23	86.51	101.71	103.20	131.29	42.55	38.64	45.22
Average benefits awarded during period											
1940	$22.71	$12.15	$10.60	$12.46	$19.60	$20.36	$13.09	—	—	—	—
1945	25.11	13.04	12.23	12.68	19.85	20.17	13.10	—	—	—	—

1950 (Jan.-Aug.)	29.03	15.02	14.08	14.35	22.65	21.65	14.65	—	—	—	—
1950 (Sept.-Dec.) [9]	33.24	19.72	11.22	27.95	35.42	36.89	37.99	—	—	—	—
1955	69.74	35.72	23.09	40.26	53.08	49.67	54.73	—	—	—	—
1960	81.73	40.25	30.37	50.87	65.93	62.10	70.14	$91.16	$35.38	$30.25	—
1961 (Jan.-July)	80.17	40.19	28.79	52.59	61.06	62.15	70.33	90.76	33.59	28.88	—
1961 (Aug.-Dec.) [10]	75.33	37.68	23.98	52.79	60.54	69.20	75.97	91.95	33.67	28.31	—
1962	78.80	39.18	27.10	53.34	61.14	70.49	77.84	92.71	33.56	28.15	—
1963	80.30	39.75	28.78	53.20	61.34	71.59	78.44	94.40	33.99	28.40	—
1964	81.24	39.92	28.59	53.20	61.31	73.06	80.21	94.98	34.22	28.66	—
1965 (Jan.-Aug.)	82.69	40.52	29.07	53.55	61.65	73.80	80.59	93.26	33.93	28.07	—
1965 (Sept.-Dec.) [11]	89.20	43.74	40.40	67.95	68.03	75.36	85.77	101.30	36.82	35.07	$33.55
1966	93.75	44.84	38.19	63.34	67.96	74.16	83.10	101.40	35.75	32.95	33.56
1967	89.74	43.04	36.93	63.75	69.24	77.67	86.13	101.84	36.35	33.05	33.87
1968 (Jan.-Feb.)	93.49	45.15	39.67	64.81	70.47	79.02	88.13	102.69	36.64	33.53	—
1968 (Mar.-Dec.) [12]	103.82	49.00	40.90	67.70	75.30	88.69	98.44	115.67	38.85	34.85	38.99
1969	106.12	50.14	41.59	69.59	75.39	90.26	100.40	118.32	39.61	35.20	39.16
1970	119.67	55.81	44.81	77.65	84.83	102.05	112.68	135.76	40.07	36.67	43.68

[1] Persons aged 65 and over (and aged 62-64, beginning 1956 for women and 1961 for men). [2] Includes, beginning 1950, wife beneficiaries under age 65 with entitled children in their care and, beginning September 1965, entitled divorced wives. [3] Includes, beginning 1957, disabled persons aged 18 and over whose disability began before age 18 and, beginning September 1965, entitled full-time students aged 18-21. [4] Includes, beginning 1950, surviving divorced mothers with entitled children in their care. [5] Includes, beginning September 1965, widows aged 60-61 and entitled surviving divorced wives aged 60 and over and, beginning March 1968, disabled widows (aged 50-59) and widowers (aged 50-61). [6] July 1957-October 1960, disabled workers aged 50-64; beginning November 1960, disabled workers under age 65. [7] Includes wife beneficiaries under age 65 with entitled children in their care and, beginning September 1965, entitled divorced wives. [8] Authorized by 1966 legislation for persons aged 72 and over not insured under the regular or transitional provisions of the Social Security Act. [9] Incorporates the effects of the 1950 amendments. [10] Incorporates the effects of the 1961 amendments. [11] Incorporates the effects of the 1965 amendments. [12] Incorporates the effects of the 1967 amendments.

Source: *Social Security Bulletin* (April 1971), Table M-13, p. 51.

Table 6

OLD AGE AND SURVIVORS INSURANCE TRUST FUND

Year	Receipts [1] (in millions)	Net Addition to Trust Fund (in millions)	Ratio of Net Change in Trust Fund to Receipts	Total Assets of Trust Fund (in millions)
1937	$ 767	$ 766	99.9%	$ 766
1938	375	366	97.6	1,132
1939	607	592	97.5	1,724
1940	368	307	83.4	2,031
1941	845	731	86.5	2,762
1942	1,085	926	85.3	3,688
1943	1,328	1,132	85.2	4,820
1944	1,422	1,185	83.3	6,005
1945	1,420	1,116	78.6	7,121
1946	1,447	1,029	71.1	8,150
1947	1,722	1,210	70.3	9,360
1948	1,969	1,362	69.2	10,722
1949	1,816	1,094	60.2	11,816
1950	2,928	1,905	65.1	13,721
1951	3,784	1,819	48.1	15,540
1952	4,184	1,902	45.5	17,442
1953	4,359	1,265	29.0	18,707
1954	5,610	1,869	33.3	20,576
1955	6,167	1,087	17.6	21,663
1956	6,697	856	12.8	22,519
1957	7,381	—126	—1.7	22,393
1958	8,117	—529	—6.5	21,864
1959	8,584	—1,723	—20.1	20,141
1960	11,382	183	1.6	20,324
1961	11,833	—599	—5.1	19,725
1962	12,585	—1,388	—11.0	18,337
1963	15,063	143	.9	18,480
1964	16,258	645	4.0	19,125
1965	16,610	—890	—5.4	18,235
1966	21,302	2,335	11.0	20,570
1967	24,034	3,652	15.2	24,222
1968	25,040	1,482	5.9	25,704
1969	29,554	4,378	14.8	30,082
1970	32,220	2,372	7.4	32,454

[1] Includes tax collections plus interest and profits.

Source: Based on *Social ·Security Bulletin, Annual Statistical Supplement*, 1969, Table 28, and 1956, Table 9; *Social Security Bulletin* (April 1971), Table M-5.

NOTES

[1] These figures refer only to OASDHI (monthly and lump-sum retirement, disability and survivors' benefits, as well as hospital and medical insurance for the aged) and state unemployment insurance; they exclude railroad and public employee retirement, veterans' benefits, workmen's compensation and public assistance.

[2] To keep the discussion manageable, I shall henceforth confine myself largely to the old age and survivors program, which accounted in 1970 for 68 percent of the benefits paid and for 85 percent of the beneficiaries.

[3] J. A. Pechman, H. J. Aaron, and M. K. Taussig, *Social Security, Perspectives for Reform* (Washington: Brookings Institution, 1968), p. 69.

[4] For a recent excellent discussion, see John A. Brittain, "The Incidence of Social Security Payroll Taxes," *American Economic Review*, LXI (March 1971), pp. 110-25.

Brittain remarks: "The Social Security Administration has been adamant in its belief that the employer tax should not be imputed to employees in comparing lifetime taxes and benefits under the social security system." (pp. 110-11.) He goes on later to say: "It is difficult to understand the position of the Social Security Administration which has conceded that this tax [the employer tax] is largely borne by labor in the aggregate and yet ignores it in evaluating the tax paid by individuals. It does so on the ground that no exact imputation of the tax is possible. However, if it is paid by employees as a group, it must also be paid by them as individuals, and it seems better to make imperfect imputations which are roughly right than to settle for being precisely wrong." (p. 123.)

[5] The one significant difference is that the employee does not have to include the employer tax in his income subject to personal income tax but does have to include the employee tax. However, this simply means that the employee tax is in fact heavier than its nominal rate. Correct analysis would treat the effective employee tax as the tax levied explicitly, plus that part of the employee's income tax attributable to the employee tax. This item too has been completely neglected by the Social Security Administration and the proponents of social security in comparing benefits and payments, still further biasing their comparisons.

[6] The exception is for persons over 72 who were not covered.

[7] It is not clear just what the right number is. Benefits are based on the "average monthly wage," which is the average of monthly wages on which social security taxes have been paid since 1951, excluding five years of lowest wages, but including months with zero wages in excess of the five years allowed. For someone who retired January 1, 1971, the maximum average monthly wage is $460 (maximum tax base since 1951 leaving out years 1951 through 1955 as the five years of lowest wages). The minimum average monthly wage sufficient to qualify at age 65 in 1971 is $5.56 a month for men and even less for women (for men, $50 a quarter for 20 quarters and no other income in the years since 1951; for women, $50 per quarter for only 17 quarters).

[8] Pechman, Aaron, and Taussig, *op. cit.*, pp. 1 and 69.

[9] See Colin D. and Rosemary G. Campbell, "Cost-Benefit Ratios under the Federal Old-Age Insurance Program," in Joint Economic Committee, *Old Age Income Assurance,* Compendium of Papers on Problems and Policy Issues in the Public and Private Pension System, Part III: *Public Programs*, pp. 72-84. 90th Cong., 1st Sess. (Washington: Government Printing Office, 1967).

[10] See Pechman, Aaron, and Taussig, *op. cit.*, pp. 82-91.

[11] *Ibid.*, p. 77.

[12] *Ibid.*, p. 75, pp. 73-74.

[13] See James Buchanan, "Social Insurance in a Growing Economy: A Proposal for Radical Reform," *National Tax Journal* (December 1968), pp. 386-95.

[14] See my columns, "Welfare: Back to the Drawing Board," *Newsweek,* May 18, 1970; and "Welfare Reform Again," *Newsweek,* September 7, 1970.

[15] See U.S. Department of Health, Education and Welfare, *Social Security Bulletin* (December 1970), p. 4. I have included in this total, which is for 1969-70, social insurance payments (except railroad retirement and public employee retirement), and public aid, civilian hospital and medical programs, maternal and child health programs, public housing, and "other social welfare." I have added food stamps and agricultural benefits. I have omitted all veterans programs, education expenditures and most health and medical programs.

[16] See Milton Friedman, *Capitalism and Freedom* (Chicago: University of Chicago Press, 1962), pp. 190-195; "The Case for the Negative Income Tax: A View from the Right," talk given at National Symposium on Guaranteed Income, sponsored by Chamber of Commerce of the United States (Washington, D.C.), December 9, 1966; "The Case for the Negative Income Tax," *Republican Papers,* ed. Melvin R. Laird (Garden City, New York: Anchor Books, 1968).

[17] James M. Buchanan and Colin D. Campbell, "Voluntary Social Security," *Wall Street Journal,* December 20, 1966.

[18] George J. Stigler, "Director's Law of Public Income Redistribution," *Journal of Law and Economics* (April 1970), p. 1.

DATE DUE

OCT 1 '76			
3 78			
NOV 1 2 1981			
FEB 3 1983			
APR 1 4 1988			
DEC 1 5 1995			

HIGHSMITH 45-220